Today's Debates

INCARCERATION

Punishment or Rehabilitation?

Erin L. McCoy and Jeff Burlingame

Cavendish
Square

New York

Published in 2020 by Cavendish Square Publishing, LLC
243 5th Avenue, Suite 136, New York, NY 10016

Library of Congress Cataloging-in-Publication Data

Names: Burlingame, Jeff, author. | McCoy, Erin L., author.
Title: Incarceration : punishment or rehabilitation? / Jeff Burlingame and
Erin L. McCoy.
Description: New York : Cavendish Square, [2019] | Series: Today's debates |
Audience: Grade level 7-12. | Includes bibliographical references and index.
Identifiers: LCCN 2018057048 (print) | LCCN 2019006846 (ebook) | ISBN
9781502644824 (ebook) | ISBN 9781502644817 (library bound) | ISBN 9781502644800 (pbk.)
Subjects: LCSH: Prisons--United States--History. | Punishment--United
States--History. | Criminals--Rehabilitation--United States--History.
Classification: LCC HV9466 (ebook) | LCC HV9466 .B853 2019 (print) | DDC
365/.973--dc23
LC record available at https://lccn.loc.gov/2018057048

Editorial Director: David McNamara
Copy Editor: Michele Suchomel-Casey
Associate Art Director: Alan Sliwinski
Designer: Christina Shults
Production Coordinator: Karol Szymczuk
Photo Research: J8 Media

CONTENTS

INTRODUCTION

The role of prisons in American society has undergone several dramatic shifts over the history of the country. So, too, have opinions about what role prisons should play and what their responsibilities are toward the people incarcerated within them.

Some argue that the primary—or even the only—purpose of a prison is to punish people for committing sometimes-horrendous crimes. They might say that prisons should rightfully be inhospitable and uncaring places so that the punishment fits the crime. Others, however, argue that people often commit crimes such as theft or drug trafficking because of underlying personal, emotional, or socioeconomic problems, and that prisons should

Opposite: An inmate is housed in the Men's Central Jail in Los Angeles, California, in 2014. Since California passed Proposition 47, fewer people are housed in the state's prisons.

offer inmates opportunities for treatment and self-improvement to prevent them from falling back into the same cycle of crime when they're released.

A Troubled System

There's a reason why such questions are so important in the United States today. Hundreds of years after the first American prison opened its doors, the United States incarcerates more people than any other country in the world. In fact, while only 5 percent of the global population lives in the United States, the nation houses 21 percent of the world's prison population, according to the National Association for the Advancement of Colored People (NAACP). A stunning 2.7 percent of all American adults are in the correctional system. That's one in every thirty-seven adults.

What's more, many have argued that unjust practices form an integral part of the criminal justice system in the United States, causing a disproportionate number of people of color to be imprisoned and making them more likely to receive longer sentences than whites. Although about 32 percent of people living in the United States are Hispanic or African American, 56 percent of all people who are incarcerated are from these demographics. In fact, African Americans are imprisoned at five times the rate of whites, and more children of color are arrested than white children.

Such high incarceration rates are very expensive to maintain. In the state of Nevada, it costs $22,000 per year to house just one inmate. In California, it costs more than $26,000 per person. If only for this reason alone, many insist that the United States needs to reduce its prison populations.

Some argue for changes in legislation to reduce or eliminate sentences for certain types of crimes. One argument that has helped lead to the legalization of marijuana in several US states has been that it would reduce the number of people in jail for cannabis-related crimes. Others say that the answer is offering rehabilitation programs to help drug-addicted inmates recover or to help inmates attain higher education levels. Such programs, much of the data shows, can make former inmates more likely to get jobs when they're released, reducing recidivism—the return to prison for committing new crimes.

Some, however, insist that rehabilitation programs such as these offer benefits to prisoners in a context in which they should be punished. What's more, they say, reducing prison sentences for certain crimes leaves more criminals on the streets, endangering public welfare.

The Changing Role of Prisons

Though the principal job of early prisons was to punish criminals, reformers eventually began to change that mission. One way they did so was by referring to prisons as correctional institutions, a much softer term, suggesting a place of treatment rather than a place of punishment. Other reforms followed. By the end of the nineteenth century, a juvenile justice system had been created that was dedicated to rehabilitating young offenders in reform schools.

However, over the past forty years, the pendulum has swung back toward where it was in the country's earliest days. Prisons have, in the past few decades, been widely focused on punishment and retribution. The shift was due in large part to a rise in the violent crime rate and a September 1971 incident that—thanks to the immediacy of television—alerted much of the United States to what life in prison was really like: the riot at Attica Correctional Facility in New York began with a prison uprising sparked by poor living conditions and ended five days later following the deaths of thirty-two prisoners and eleven guards who had been taken hostage. However, this shift in how prisons were run was

A corridor in the Attica Correctional Facility in New York is littered with debris after a violent prison riot in September 1971.

also triggered by a very different impression that was widespread among the public: many thought that being in prison was not a big deal and was not that much of a punishment.

The Attica incident was the bloodiest prison battle in American history, and its impact extended far beyond the prison walls. A majority of Americans soon called for tougher laws that would put criminals behind bars for longer periods of time. Many of these criminals were drug users who swelled the inmate ranks. Supporters claim that lengthy prison sentences have cut down the rate of violent crime, which fell to historic lows in the

2000s. Others disagree, claiming that the lower crime rates were the result of better policing and better citizen management of behaviors such as drunk driving and leaving doors unlocked.

Meanwhile, as prisons overflow, state budgets are breaking under the weight of huge correctional expenditures. Reductions in expenditures have impacted conditions inside prisons, and there are debates over the quality of health care and vocational training, the levels of violence, the treatment of undocumented immigrants, and the treatment of juvenile offenders.

While some continue to insist that prisons need to limit themselves to their original intent of punishing criminals, rehabilitation programs are nevertheless becoming more common in the United States. States such as Georgia, Texas, Arkansas, Hawaii, Kentucky, and Ohio have instituted wide-ranging reforms, including "drug courts" designed to treat drug-addicted offenders rather than send them to prison. In October 2018, the state of Louisiana announced it would invest nearly $7 million in education and rehabilitation. A month later, US president Donald Trump backed a bill, the First Step Act, that would reduce prison sentences for some while creating rehabilitation and vocational programs. The bill appeared to have bipartisan support in the US Congress.

A View of the GUARD-HOUSE and SIMSBURY-M
now called Newgate,
A Prison for the Confinement of Loyalists in Connect

Chapter One

A HISTORY OF AMERICAN PRISONS

Twenty-five feet (7.6 meters) under the ground, accessible only by rope or ladder, dank and awful-smelling caverns, former mine shafts, housed one of the earliest—and most notorious—prisons in US history. Water dripped from the ceilings. A former prisoner recalled that "armies of fleas, lice, and bedbugs covered every inch of the floor which itself was covered in 5 inches [12.7 centimeters] of slippery, stinking filth." Year-round, the temperature below hovered around an uncomfortable 50 degrees Fahrenheit (10 degrees Celsius).

As reported by writer W. Storrs Lee and the Connecticut Humanities Council, such were the conditions in the earliest days of Newgate Prison in Simsbury, Connecticut. The prison—located in an

Opposite: The guardhouse and mine that became Connecticut's Newgate Prison are shown in a diagram. The prison housed inmates in a former mine shaft 25 feet (7.6 meters) underground.

abandoned copper mine where British prisoners had been kept during the American Revolution—first opened its doors in 1773 as the colony's option for housing serious criminals and became a state prison in 1790. Prisoners at Newgate were subjected to violence and were poorly fed. They would eventually stage the first prison riot in American history.

Although conditions faced by prisoners at Newgate may sound unusually harsh, they were not atypical for the time. Similar conditions had existed for centuries in European prisons, although that began to change shortly after Newgate came into existence.

Early American Prisons

Led by lecturer and reformer John Howard, a prison reform movement was underway in England around the same time that Newgate was accepting its first prisoners. With Howard's help, the British had begun to recognize that prisoners might change their lives if they were treated more humanely. Howard saw prisons as places where criminals might do penance for their crimes, recognize their sinful ways, and reform. He used the word "penitentiary" to describe the type of prison he had in mind, and he wrote the Penitentiary Act, which was passed by the British Parliament in 1779. The act helped improve conditions for prisoners based on religious tenets and focused on their rehabilitation in addition to their punishment.

Howard's reforms were put to the test in 1785, at a jail that opened at Wymondham in Norfolk, England. Instead of housing all prisoners together, as had been the norm, male and female criminals were confined separately at Wymondham. Prisoners were also placed in separate cells where they could have time to think about their crimes and do penance for them so they could transform their lives.

In the United States, Howard's reforms were adopted in 1790 in Philadelphia at the Walnut Street Jail. The jail used the "Pennsylvania" system of prison reform. Inmates were kept in solitary confinement in separate cells, where they were expected to read the Bible and repent for their crimes. At first, they were given nothing to do but those tasks, but gradually they were given work, such as shoe-making and chair-making, to keep them busy. Since each prisoner worked, ate, and slept in his or her cell, the cells had to be fairly large, which meant each correctional institution could house only a small prison population. Western State Penitentiary, which opened in Pittsburgh, Pennsylvania, in 1826, also adopted this system, as did Eastern State Penitentiary, which opened in Philadelphia in 1829.

An alternative to the Pennsylvania system was initiated in 1821 at a prison in Auburn, New York. Under the "Auburn" system, prisoners slept in separate cells but worked and ate together in large common rooms. In these areas, they were not permitted to talk to each other. At Auburn, long cell blocks with small individual cells were constructed, enabling each prison to house a larger population than under the Pennsylvania system. When prison authorities discovered that it was more efficient to have prisoners work together, and learned that they produced far more this way, the Auburn system gradually became the model for most US prisons. Since the products produced by inmates could be sold outside the prison, the profits could be used to pay for much of the cost of running the correctional institutions where they were made. Prisoners were now helping to pay for their own upkeep.

New prisons based on the Auburn system soon sprang up. In the late 1820s, the Sing Sing prison opened in Ossining, New York. A year prior, the Wethersfield State Prison had opened in Wethersfield, Connecticut. Many other states soon opened prisons

Ex-slaves are depicted working on a cotton plantation. Even after emancipation, African American prisoners were forced to work for free.

of their own. In fact, between 1825 and 1870, twenty-three prisons based on the Auburn system opened. Gradually, the system's rule of silence was ended, and prisoners were permitted to speak to each other.

Nevertheless, conditions inside the prisons remained harsh. Each prisoner wore a striped suit that identified him or her as a convicted felon. If prisoners did not follow the rules, they were severely disciplined. That could mean they were saddled with a ball and chain wrapped around their body to prevent escape and ease of movement, were whipped by prison guards, or were placed for many hours in pillories, wooden frames with holes for a prisoner's head and hands.

In some states, prisoners were regularly leased out to private contractors to do a variety of work. Shackled together in what was called a chain gang, they worked at building railroads, repairing roadways, or doing plantation work.

After the country's slaves were freed following the American Civil War, African Americans were still not treated fairly. They were often treated badly and arrested if they were suspected of not having jobs or of committing a minor crime, such as fighting or petty theft. As *The American Prison* explains, "Instead of being punished on plantations, former slaves were jammed into overcrowded, dilapidated correctional facilities." Many of them were sent out to farms where they picked cotton, cut sugarcane, and harvested vegetables. As such, many African Americans were forced to go right back to doing what they had done before they had been freed.

Prisoners were brought to plantations in mobile cages that housed up to thirty people. These African American prisoners worked long hours, with little to eat, and received severe punishment if they misbehaved. "Humane treatment of prisoners … took a back seat to profit making," *The American Prison* states.

Early Prison Reform

During the last quarter of the nineteenth century, a reform movement swept across the United States that affected many parts of American society, including state prisons. The United States' vast industrialization had created large manufacturing plants, enormous mining operations, and sprawling cities. Working conditions in the factories and mines were often dangerous, while in cities, hundreds of thousands of workers lived in crowded and unsanitary slums. Large numbers of foreigners who had entered the cities in search of factory work had found none. Rather than retreating to their homelands of China, Ireland, and Italy, these jobless people remained in the cities and lived in the slums. Such areas became hotbeds for crime.

A group of reformers began to investigate these conditions and write about them in popular magazines. They also focused on the treatment of prisoners inside America's correctional institutions—including the harsh punishments meted out to prisoners, the inadequate food, and overcrowding.

During the remainder of the nineteenth century, more prisons continued to be built as the prison population increased. In 1850, there were 30 prisoners for every 100,000 Americans. By 1900, this number had more than doubled to 75 per 100,000.

Even as the population swelled, the prison system continued to operate under the premise that incarceration was meant to punish. But there was a small group of reformers who thought that prisons should be dedicated to transforming prisoners and changing their lives.

In 1870, that prison reform movement gathered momentum with the founding of the National Prison Association, later called the American Correctional Association. Ohio governor Rutherford B. Hayes—who later was elected president of the United States—became head of the new association. Hayes called on prison leaders nationwide to institute reforms that would provide more humane treatment of prisoners, offer them education and job training, and put an end to fixed sentences, which had been popular at the time. Such sentences stated an exact amount of time a prisoner had to spend behind bars, without exception. In their stead came indeterminate sentences, in which judges sentenced criminals to a range of time behind bars. This allowed for some flexibility about when the criminals were released, based on factors such as how much they had reformed while in prison.

The meeting of the National Prison Association led to the establishment of a new correctional facility at Elmira, New York, which was directed by Zebulon Brockway. The Elmira Reformatory, which opened in 1876, housed younger prisoners, ages sixteen to thirty, who were serving their first prison terms.

Key Criminal Justice Terminology

The various levels of the criminal justice system in America can be summed up with one key point: it's all a matter of degree.

In most places, criminal courts—and places to keep accused and convicted criminals—are set up at different levels that depend on the severity of the crime. Criminal courts are distinct from civil courts, which are set up to decide lawsuits.

District courts are usually associated with city jails. These will try the least severe crimes, from traffic offenses to shoplifting, and will sometimes try more severe crimes depending on where the crime was committed and the resources of the law enforcement agencies involved.

City jails generally serve to keep convicted criminals whose sentences are less than thirty days and are also used to hold accused criminals while they are on trial. In fact, many cities and towns have combined their court and jail into one building so that a prisoner can simply be transferred from a cell in one part of the building to a courtroom in another part.

County and parish jails are usually associated with superior courts, which try cases up to and including murder. These are usually more secure facilities that hold inmates whose sentences range up to one year.

What is generally referred to as a prison usually is a much larger and more secure state or federal facility. Prisons hold inmates with much longer sentences, including life sentences. In states where the death penalty is used, one prison will often be designated for death row. This holds inmates who have been sentenced to death.

Most states maintain their own prison systems. The federal government also maintains a network of prisons, including the supermaxes—super-maximum-security prisons where the most infamous of criminals are kept.

At Elmira, young offenders had the opportunity to receive an education and learn a vocational trade, such as knitting or shoemaking, so they could lead successful lives in the community after release. They also had the opportunity to receive a reduced sentence, given as a reward for those who had demonstrated good behavior. Over the next four decades, several other states opened reformatories based on the Elmira system.

The Elmira Reformatory also led to the establishment of a separate court system for juvenile offenders. Exactly what age constituted a juvenile varied. Sometimes, the cutoff age was sixteen or seventeen; other times, it was eighteen or even nineteen. Regardless, beginning in Chicago in 1899, this new court system permitted judges to treat young offenders differently than adults. Youths were considered to be in the formative stages of their development and therefore were not believed to be as responsible as adults for any crimes that they may have committed. Judges could put them on probation for minor crimes such as vandalism, simple assault, and petty theft. This meant the offender did not receive a prison sentence, but rather supervision by officers of the court. Meanwhile, the first juvenile prison opened at St. Charles, Illinois, in 1904. For the first time, juveniles found to have committed criminal offenses were placed in a separate institution—not in the same prison as adults.

At the same time, separate female prisons were also being constructed. The first was the Female Prison and Reformatory Institution for Girls and Women in Indianapolis, Indiana, in 1874. Another female prison opened in 1877 at Sherborn, Massachusetts. These prisons were significant because they allowed women to escape the sexual abuse many of them had been subjected to during the time they were locked up with men.

Parole, used extensively at Elmira, became a key element of the entire American prison system. This concept had been pioneered in Australia by Alexander Maconochie, head of that

Prisoners at the Elmira Reformatory attend lessons in 1913. The innovative facility offered offenders the chance to receive an education and learn a trade.

country's Norfolk Island prison. Maconochie had established a "mark system," enabling prisoners who acted responsibly to earn good marks, or good-time credits, that would shorten their sentences. The mark system acted as an incentive for prisoners to behave themselves while they were behind bars. Meanwhile, an Irish reformer named Sir Walter Crofton had instituted the "ticket-of-leave" system in Ireland. This system enabled prisoners to pass through a series of stages based on good behavior. Those stages began with solitary confinement and progressed to work in the outside community without supervision. Prisoners who performed well at each stage could be given a pardon, or ticket of leave, and win an early release from prison.

The Prison System Expands

Though reform was instituted in some prisons, most facilities continued to treat inmates harshly. As stated in *The American Prison*, overall prison life during the first quarter of the twentieth century continued to be characterized by "total control, punishment and hard labor." There were few opportunities for prisoners to receive an education. Medical treatment for illness or injury was not adequate, and punishment for prisoners who disobeyed the rules was severe. Stephen Cox, author of a book on the history of American prisons, *The Big House*, writes: "If you live in a nineteenth-century prison … you may be locked in a dark cell and kept there on rations of bread and water. You may be forced to take down your pants so you can be paddled like a schoolboy. You may be put in a cell with your wrists chained to the bars, and your nose pointed at a solid steel outer door … and be left there to stand for hours at a time." Regardless of how brutal such treatment may sound today, this was still acceptable to a majority of Americans at the time.

As prison populations continued to swell, more prisons were built. Between 1900 and 1925, thirty-one major prisons for adults were constructed nationwide. Meanwhile, the federal government had also begun constructing prisons to house criminals convicted of federal crimes, such as kidnapping and counterfeiting. Previously, federal prisoners had been held in state-run prisons, but that changed in 1887 after Congress prohibited federal prisoners from being used as workers for outside businesses. State prisons could no longer contract out their federal inmates and profit from their work, so they did not want to pay for their upkeep. Thus, a need arose for a system in which to house federal prisoners. In 1906, the first US penitentiary opened at Fort Leavenworth, Kansas. Federal prisons in Atlanta, Georgia, and on McNeil Island, Washington, followed. In 1930, the Federal

Bureau of Prisons was established to oversee all eleven of the federal prisons in existence at the time.

Many of these prisons held people who had been convicted of violating prohibition laws, including the Eighteenth Amendment, which came into effect in 1920. These laws prevented the manufacture, sale, and transport of alcohol. However, prohibition was widely violated, especially by gangsters who realized that they could grow wealthy supplying alcohol to the millions of Americans who still wanted to drink. Bootlegging—the illegal manufacture and sale of alcohol—also led to violent conflicts between gangs of mobsters who tried to control the illegal alcohol industry. A similar situation exists today in the world of illegal drugs.

While the prison population was increasing, the jobs that prisoners were allowed to perform changed. In 1929, Congress passed the Hawes-Cooper Act, giving each state the right to prevent items from crossing its borders if those items were made in prisons located in other states. The act was passed because, thanks to free labor, convict-made goods were much cheaper than those goods produced by companies that used non-convict workers. Labor unions had huge problems with this competition.

The Hawes-Cooper Act was strengthened in 1935 and again in 1940. As a result, prison work declined, leaving many prisoners with little to do while they were behind bars. During World War II, this law was temporarily relaxed so that prisoners could make clothing and other items necessary to support American soldiers in combat. For example, shoes and boots were produced by prisoners at Fort Leavenworth, while aircraft engines were manufactured by prisoners at the Federal Reformatory in Chillicothe, Ohio.

Changes After World War II

After World War II, a new reform movement began to again transform America's prisons. This coincided with advancements in the field of psychology that helped people to effectively deal with emotional problems. As the Joint Commission on Correctional Manpower and Training reported in 1970, "The offender was perceived as a person with social, intellectual, or emotional deficiencies who should be diagnosed carefully and his deficiencies clinically defined. Programs should be designed to correct these deficiencies to the point that would permit him to assume a productive, law-abiding place in the community." It was at this point that people began referring to prisons as "correctional institutions."

Prison health care soon began to improve. In addition, prisoners entering a correctional facility were diagnosed more carefully and separated from each other according to their diagnosed mental illnesses. New diagnostic centers opened at locations such as Menlo Park, New Jersey, to test and evaluate entering prisoners. These facilities reflected advances in psychiatry and the understanding of mental illness that occurred during the twentieth century.

New prison facilities were also built to house prisoners who had committed different types of crimes. For example, maximum-security prisons—today known as supermax prisons—housed violent criminals, such as serial murderers and gang leaders. Prisoners there were kept locked in their cells, a condition called lockdown, for most of the day. Medium-security prisons housed inmates who had committed less-severe crimes. There, prisoners often slept in dormitories that were locked at night, ate in dining halls, and bathed in communal showers. Minimum-security prisons housed prisoners who had been convicted of so-called white-collar crimes, such as embezzling money and nonviolent drug-related crimes. Since they were considered to pose little threat to society, these prisoners might have minimal supervision and might even be assigned to work on community projects.

Rioters at the Attica Correctional Facility in 1971 rally for better living conditions and speak out against the guards' alleged racial prejudice.

Unfortunately, the increase in prison construction could not keep pace with the growing prisoner population and the problem of overcrowding. This was, in part, because of the growth of the illegal drug trade in the United States, as more people began using such substances as cocaine. In 1971, President Richard Nixon declared a war on drugs, and drug-related arrests increased. By the mid-1970s, more than two hundred thousand people were incarcerated, nearly double the figure of just fifty years earlier.

Severe overcrowding was one of the factors that led to the brutal prison riot at the Attica Correctional Facility in New York in 1971. Prisoners there also complained about poor living conditions and racial prejudice by white guards toward black inmates. Overcrowding, along with poor sanitation and other factors, also played a key role in another severe riot, which broke out at the New Mexico State Penitentiary in 1980. That gruesome uprising resulted in the death of thirty-three prisoners.

Some people argued that these events indicated that prison conditions were still in need of reform. Others argued that prisons in fact were not tough enough and that prisoners needed to be placed under stronger restraints. One former prison aide told investigators after the New Mexico riot, "That prison was the most corrupt place on earth. I lived in fear of dying, because I knew that if I died while I worked in that place, I'd go straight to hell."

Defining Prisoners' Rights

Prison inmates have some, but not all, of the same constitutional rights as other American citizens. For instance, inmates are not permitted to vote in elections, based on the theory that those people who are not able to follow the law should not be allowed to help choose those who make it.

The US Supreme Court, in a series of decisions in the 1970s, defined the way that the US Constitution protects the rights of

American prisoners. In 1974, Justice Byron White wrote the majority opinion in the case of *Wolff v. McDonnell* regarding a prisoner's right to retain or lose good-time credits that would shorten his or her sentence based on good behavior while behind bars. Charles Wolff Jr. and other prisoners in Nebraska claimed they had lost their good-time credits without due process of law—that is, the same procedures that other citizens living outside prison would have received. The court determined that inmates are sometimes entitled to due process, depending on several factors, such as how serious the misconduct was.

In another case decided in 1974, *Procunier v. Martinez*, Justice William Powell delivered the majority opinion of the Supreme Court regarding mail censorship in prison. The court ruled that prison administrators could not prevent a prisoner from receiving mail because that would violate the protection of free speech contained in the Bill of Rights of the Constitution. Only mail that might undermine prison security or the rehabilitation of inmates can be censored. Determination of such is made by prison staff who open and examine the mail before distributing it.

In 1976, in *Estelle v. Gamble*, Justice Thurgood Marshall addressed medical care for prisoners. He wrote, "Deliberate indifference by prison personnel to a prisoner's serious illness or injury constitutes cruel and unusual punishment." This is a violation of the Eighth Amendment to the Constitution.

There have been many tough-on-crime laws that have taken away prisoners' rights as well, beginning in the 1980s, when a conservative Supreme Court was in place. In 1981, for example, in the case of *Rhodes v. Chapman*, the Supreme Court ruled in a majority decision written by Justice Powell that overcrowding is not unconstitutional. "The Constitution does not mandate comfortable prisons," Justice Powell concluded. In 1984, the court ruled that the Fourth Amendment does not apply to prisoners. Therefore, they can be subject to searches and seizures of their property. In

1995, the Prison Litigation Reform Act placed limitations on how much prisoners could complain about conditions in their prisons and made it harder for prisoners to file federal lawsuits. In 2009, the Supreme Court denied prisoners the right to use DNA testing in an attempt to prove their innocence after they had been found guilty. The court said it was up to individual states to decide their own policies on the matter.

One of the biggest decisions by the Supreme Court came in 2010. It stated that, upon being arrested, once criminal suspects have been read their rights—known as Miranda rights—they must speak up to invoke those rights. Therefore, if they wish to remain silent or have an attorney present during their questioning, they must say so, otherwise whatever they tell police can be used against them later during any subsequent trials for their crime. Prior to the Supreme Court's 1966 decision in *Miranda v. Arizona*, police could question suspects as much as they wanted and pressure them into admitting to crimes. Miranda laws gave suspects more power during their initial questioning, but the 2010 ruling took back some of that power.

Other major recent Supreme Court decisions have abolished the death penalty for juvenile offenders, ruled that sex offenders can continue to be housed in general prisons, and barred life sentences without parole for juvenile offenders for crimes other than murder.

Reforms Continue

During the American colonial period, towns built jails to house prisoners who were awaiting corporal punishment—the infliction of painful measures, such as whipping or beating, on someone for disciplinary purposes. Today, corporal punishment may be considered inhumane by certain societies, but it was the norm at the time, being imposed even for minor crimes such as public intoxication.

However, as corporal punishment disappeared around the end of the eighteenth century, local governments began constructing prisons to house criminals who were sentenced to spend time behind bars. During the nineteenth century, prisoners received training in various trades so they could lead successful lives in the community. Near the end of that century, a system of parole was introduced to reward prisoners who had demonstrated good behavior with release dates before their sentences were completed. Still, during the first quarter of the twentieth century, prison life continued to be perceived as a place where punishment was the first priority.

After World War II, prisons grew larger and larger. In time, prison became known, in slang, as "the Big House." Many Americans continued to believe that the primary task of prisons was to punish convicted criminals for their crimes. However, during the prosperous post-war years, sentiment was with those reformers who believed that prisons should be dedicated to transforming prisoners and changing their lives.

Today, after the high incarceration rates created by the war on drugs, mandatory minimum sentences, and other factors, the pendulum is swinging once again, back toward a system that incorporates rehabilitation for the incarcerated. More and more states are adopting such measures as the data suggests that it reduces both costs and incarceration rates.

Chapter Two

CHALLENGES AND CONTROVERSIES IN US PRISONS

As the adoption of **rehabilitation programs** becomes more widespread, states have begun to share pivotal data around the success of such efforts. For instance, the state of Ohio, which has a reincarceration rate of 40 percent among released prisoners, has found that inmates who enroll in college courses during their time in prison have a reincarceration rate of just 18 percent. Similarly, education programs reduced Nevada's prison population by 1.6 percent, saving the state $38 million and making the construction of $1.2 billion in new facilities unnecessary. Minnesota started a work-release program that between 2007 and 2011 saved $1.25 million, and vocational programs

Opposite: At the March for Justice in Harlem, New York City, on August 26, 2017, protesters call for prison reform.

there led to better jobs for—and increased tax revenues from—released prisoners.

These are just a few examples of what recent reforms have accomplished. Some, however, argue that many of these reforms should be approached with caution or that they are outright ineffective. Arkansas senator Tom Cotton, for example, has pointed to the recidivism problem as evidence that sentences shouldn't be shortened, since some people are "not prepared to re-enter society." In the face of a 2016 bill to reduce mandatory minimum sentences, which set minimum amounts of prison time for certain crimes, Cotton declared that the United States in fact suffered from an "under-incarceration problem."

Likewise, noted criminologist Charles H. Logan, author of *Private Prisons: Cons and Pros*, has argued:

> *Prisons should not try to be "correctional institutions" … The message of a prison should be simple: "Felonies are wrong and controllable acts, and those who commit them will be punished." Institutions aiming for "rehabilitation" more often transmit this muddled message: "Felonies are the result of social and personal deficiencies … and society has a responsibility to correct these deficiencies." … Such a message may excuse, and even encourage, crime; at the very least, it weakens the vital punishment messages of imprisonment.*

High populations, the status of juvenile justice, a controversial parole system, unequal incarceration rates for whites vs. non-whites, and poor prison conditions are all sources of heated debate around incarceration in America. Let's take a look at how these topics are playing out in the prison system today.

High Prison Populations

Over the past hundred years, the number of prisoners in correctional facilities has grown significantly. The upward trend began during the 1920s as a result of rising unemployment and violations of prohibition laws. In 1918, for example, there were approximately 82 people in prison per 100,000 Americans. By 1940, that number had risen to 132 for every 100,000 people.

Those numbers continued to grow. By the first decade of the twenty-first century, more than 700 people were in prison for every 100,000. As of 2018, there were nearly 2.3 million people behind bars in the United States, according to the Prison Policy Initiative, a nonpartisan, nonprofit organization that conducts research on mass criminalization. An estimated 615,000 American prisoners are in local jails for minor offenses such as traffic violations or awaiting trial or sentencing for more serious offenses. More than 1.5 million are in state and federal prisons, while others are in immigration detention, involuntary commitment facilities, and other types of detention.

Let's explore why prison populations have increased so much over the last century.

Truth-in-Sentencing Laws

During the early 1980s, Liam Q. served aboard an aircraft carrier in the United States Navy. While he was on shore leave in Norfolk, Virginia, he began an affair with a married woman. In 1983, at age nineteen, he was convicted of murdering the woman's husband and given a life sentence in prison. At the time, a life sentence meant that, with good behavior and the ability to show a parole board he had changed, Liam might serve only eighteen or nineteen years in prison.

Pictured here at the Buena Vista Correctional Facility in Colorado in 2015, Larry Thompson is more than twenty years into a life sentence for a murder he claims he did not commit.

About ten years later, that possibility of one day leaving prison vanished for a majority of lifers—those serving life sentences—when forty states, including Virginia, passed "truth-in-sentencing" laws, also known as determinate sentences. With regard to life sentences, the new laws meant that anyone given a life sentence would be expected to serve as much as 85 percent of it before being considered for parole. This was part of a nationwide trend to get tough with criminals brought about when advocacy groups and the public at large began to demand an ability to know exactly how long convicted criminals would be behind bars. As an extra incentive to enact these new laws, Congress passed the Violent Crime Control and Law Enforcement Act in 1994. Under this legislation, states were offered additional funds to construct new prisons if they adopted truth-in-sentencing laws.

There is little dispute that truth-in-sentencing laws and an increased number of prisoners serving life sentences are among the reasons that the prison population has soared over the past fifteen years. This increase in life sentences with little or no chance for parole also has meant that an increasing number of prisoners are middle-aged or elderly. Between 1999 and 2016, the number of inmates fifty-five or older in federal and state prisons increased by 280 percent, while the number of younger adults increased just 3 percent.

The Sentencing Project argues that long sentences may not be effective in preventing crime, as people become significantly less likely to commit crimes when they reach their thirties and forties. What's more, long sentences are expensive, in part because people tend to need more medical care as they age, so these older prisoners tend to cost taxpayers more.

Mandatory Minimums

Another factor that has led to an increase in the prison population is state legislatures' widespread adoption of mandatory minimum sentencing laws beginning in the 1970s during President Nixon's war on drugs. The new laws meant that judges no longer had wide discretion in passing sentences on convicted criminals. Instead, they were required to hand down sentences that followed the guidelines in the laws. For example, these laws require that anyone convicted of possession of 5 grams (0.18 ounces) of crack cocaine will receive a minimum sentence of five years in prison. To illustrate, 5 grams of crack cocaine is the equivalent of less than two of the sugar packets commonly found in restaurants and is good for approximately twenty-five doses, depending on the user.

As a result of mandatory sentencing laws and the war on drugs, the number of drug offenders arrested annually almost quadrupled from 1970 to about two million during the first decade of the twenty-first century. Thanks to the relative ease of catching small-time users, as well as the sheer numbers of such individuals, the vast majority of the people serving sentences are not dealers or so-called drug kingpins—gang leaders—but people caught using illegal drugs.

Three-Strikes Laws

Prison populations also have increased due to the three-strikes laws that have been passed by some states. In Washington State, for example, a third felony conviction can lead to a life sentence behind bars. Those who believe that such mandates are too strict commonly point to stories of people who have been sentenced to life in prison on the basis of rather minor crimes—people such as Mary Thompson, for example, who was convicted of stealing tracksuits from a store in 1982 to support her drug addiction. Yet because it was her third felony conviction, she received a life sentence with no chance of parole until 2020.

Despite its perceived flaws, many policymakers believe strongly that three-strikes laws are effective. R. David LaCourse Jr. is among them. As executive director of Washington Citizens for Justice, LaCourse played an integral role in drafting Washington's three-strikes law, which became the first such law in the United

States when it was enacted in 1993. Four years after the law was on the books, LaCourse wrote:

> *Many police officers, corrections officers and others, both inside and outside the criminal justice system, have noted that criminals fear Three Strikes. These people have also found that some criminals have modified their behavior. For once, felons are worried about the criminal justice system and that has proven to be a deterrent factor … Washington's Three Strikes law has worked as intended. The law is incarcerating violent, career criminals who are unlikely to change their behavior.*

Juvenile Justice

Another hotly debated issue of today is the American corrections system's treatment of juvenile offenders. Each of the fifty states has established a special court system to handle juvenile offenders under the age of eighteen. However, every state allows a juvenile accused of a violent crime to be tried as an adult in certain instances, such as if they are accused of murder. Those who are convicted under such circumstances receive adult sentences that may put them in prison for many years, even for life, though in 2010 the US Supreme Court barred life sentences for juveniles unless they had committed murder.

Like adults, juveniles sent to youth prisons, or separate facilities for juveniles, have also been subjected to harsh treatment by prison officials, according to at least one study conducted in New York. In addition, many states cut their budgets for mental health care during the Great Recession of 2007–2009. As a result, juvenile offenders with mental illness were increasingly being sent to juvenile prisons instead of being treated by community mental health facilities. Such prisons have been criticized for not having enough therapists on hand.

The US Parole System

Since the end of the nineteenth century, prisons have used parole—or early release from prison—as a way of rewarding inmates for good behavior. While tougher sentencing laws have reduced the number of parolees, convicts on parole currently number approximately 840,000. Another 3.7 million people are

A parole officer (*left*) meets with a parolee whom he oversees to make sure the latter is meeting all the requirements of his parole.

on probation, in which they are under court supervision in lieu of being sent to prison. During their probation or parole, people are often required to follow court-mandated rules, about their housing or employment situation, for instance.

The parole system is overburdened. Many parole officers already have large caseloads, which reduces the amount of attention that they can give to each parolee. Community services are also frequently inadequate in helping parolees deal with substance-abuse problems, find jobs, or locate a place to live. However, efforts are underway in many states through community agencies, churches, and other groups to help inmates after they leave prison and reenter the community. This is all aimed at reducing the rate at which parolees return to prison—called recidivism. About 76 percent of all released prisoners are rearrested within five years, according to the National Institute of Justice. The reasons for such high rates vary, but in general, proponents of rehabilitation believe that they can be traced to prisoners not receiving enough education and treatment while they are incarcerated.

Many people in positions of authority believe that taking such a stance labels the criminal a victim and unjustly blames the state for crimes committed by individuals. Dan Lungren, during his time as an attorney general of California and Republican member of Congress, believed that focusing too much on the rights of criminals undermines the entire purpose of the criminal justice system, which is to protect innocent people from crime. In 1996, Lungren wrote:

> *A criminal justice system that contorts itself to the extreme in a purported effort "to protect the accused," with the result that the innocent victim is denied justice (which includes retribution), is a system which has lost its sight and soul and forfeited its right to be*

called *"just"* or justice ... *I urge you not to forget the true victims of crime: those who have been violently assaulted by others, and the families of victims.*

Unequal Incarceration Rates

A disproportionate percentage of US prisoners are African American and other people of color. "An estimated one-third of black male Americans will spend time in state or federal prison at some point in their lifetime—more than double the rate from the 1970s and over five times higher than the rate for white males," writes Jonathan Rothwell in a 2014 article for public policy organization the Brookings Institution.

In fact, according to the Sentencing Project, in 2015 alone, one in seventeen black men and one in forty-two Hispanic men were in prison compared to one in ninety-one white men. Black women were two times more likely to be in prison than white women, and Hispanic women were 1.2 times more likely.

The war on drugs in particular has unfairly impacted people of color and especially the African American community. Whites are equally likely to use drugs and more likely to sell them than African Americans—yet, as Rothwell reports, blacks are 2.5 times more likely to be arrested for possession and 3.6 times more likely to be arrested for selling.

Many argue that one of the most compelling reasons for prison reform is that people of color and their communities are disproportionately affected. This, in the long term, leads to higher rates of poverty among these communities, a 2018 study confirms. The Stanford University study found that, even when African American boys are raised in households that are socioeconomically similar to those of white boys, the former fare worse than the latter in 99 percent of the United States. The *New York Times* elaborates:

"White boys who grow up rich are likely to remain that way. Black boys raised at the top, however, are more likely to become poor than to stay wealthy in their own adult households." Why is this? The study concludes that racism—widespread and institutionalized racism at all levels of society—is the root of the problem.

What about the 1 percent of black boys who, in the end, fared just as well as whites? There was one thing that made them different: they lived in neighborhoods where their fathers were more likely to be living at home. One in three black men spends time in prison during their lifetimes, and this absence, it seems, is having a profound intergenerational effect on African American communities. In this case, it is preventing them from rising out of poverty.

Poor Living Conditions

With nearly 2.3 million people in prison in the United States today, overcrowding and overall living conditions have become a problem in many prisons. However, this is by no means a new issue—it has in fact been growing worse for more than three decades. By 1982, forty-two states had been ordered by the federal courts to improve prison conditions because of overcrowding, poor levels of health care, deteriorating housing, and other problems. States built more prisons in an attempt to address these issues, but this often failed to help because the prison population continued to grow at the same time.

In 1975, the prison population in the United States stood at roughly 100 per 100,000. By 2018, that number had skyrocketed to 830 per 100,000—though this was still below its peak at 1,000 per 100,000 adults in 2006–2008, according to the Pew Research Center. As a result, over the last few decades, conditions have continued to deteriorate inside many prison facilities. Prisoners have complained of working for wages well

An estimated 250 inmates were injured in a 2009 prison riot in Chino, California, where an estimated 5,900 men were being held in a facility designed to house just 3,000. The aftermath of that riot is shown here.

below minimum wage, amounting to what some call "modern slavery." Others have complained about the lack of rehabilitation programs or heavy overcrowding. Many prisoners also fear for their safety. It is estimated that 200,000 people in prison are sexually assaulted each year, many by corrections staff; a vast number of these assaults go unreported.

During the Great Recession of 2007–2009, the quality of life behind bars deteriorated. Kenneth Hartman, author of *Mother California: A Story of Redemption Behind Bars*, was sentenced to life without parole for murder in 1980. In his book, he wrote that the quantity and quality of prison food—which is chock-full of potatoes and meat substitutes—markedly decreased during that time and added that even before the recession, prisoners in the California system "lost most of the positive programs, like conjugal [spousal] visits and college education that we had

had since the '70s." He added that, during the summer, the air-conditioning broke in the visiting room and 150 people had to put up with heat that regularly hits 100 degrees F (38°C).

Proponents of punishment would counter Hartman's story with the argument that life behind bars is not supposed to be filled with all the conveniences people enjoy outside prison. After all, inmates are there because they committed crimes, thereby forfeiting their right to live what might be called a "normal" life.

Many people believe that crime can only be deterred if prisons are places that people want to avoid at all costs. Former Republican congressman Richard "Dick" Zimmer of New Jersey is one of them. He said, "Some criminals have come to view jail as an almost acceptable lifestyle because amenities are better for them on the inside than on the outside. When you break the law of the land, you should pay the price for your crime, not be rewarded with a vacation watching premium cable on your personal television."

Nevertheless, prisoners are speaking out about these conditions and insisting that they are in many cases inhumane. In August 2018, prisoners in at least ten states went on strike to protest low wages. Many in California, for instance, had been recruited to fight the state's deadly wildfires. They were paid only $1 an hour plus $2 per day for this dangerous work. Many others are paid less than a dollar an hour or not paid at all for their work.

"Prisoners want to be valued as contributors to our society," said spokesperson Amani Sawari. "Every single field and industry is affected on some level by prisons, from our license plates to the fast food that we eat to the stores that we shop at. So we really need to recognize how we are supporting the prison industrial complex through the dollars that we spend."

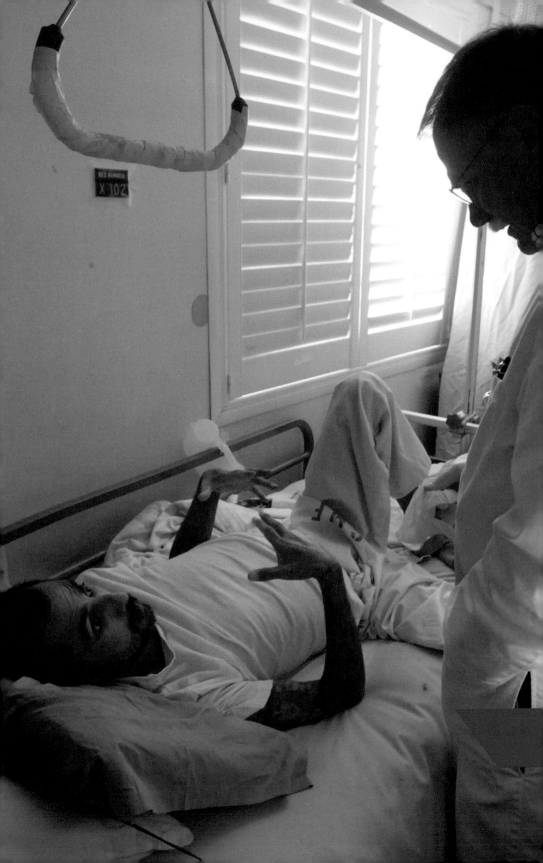

Chapter Three

EDUCATION AND HEALTH CARE

When people are given a prison sentence, they don't go straight to prison. First, they must pass through an intake system in which they are documented, fingerprinted, and photographed. This process can take under two weeks or, in some states, more than six months.

Their personal items are noted and confiscated by the staff; they are then stored in the prisoners' personal files. A team of experts at an intake facility may recommend where the inmate should serve his or her sentence—in a minimum- or maximum-security prison, for instance. This classification system is based on a set of standards that score each inmate the same way.

Opposite: Luis Duran (*left*), an inmate with cancer, is pictured in the hospice unit at a facility in Vacaville, California. He is speaking with Dr. David Mathis.

In addition, qualified medical professionals assess the mental and physical health of each inmate. This assessment includes a physical examination and an evaluation for addiction problems such as alcohol or drug abuse. This information helps determine any special health care or mental health programs that a prisoner may require while serving time in a correctional institution.

The goal is that, when prisoners are finally transferred to the prison where they will serve out their sentences, that prison will offer programs that fulfill the prisoner's needs for health care, vocational training, and education. This, however, is not always the case.

Health Care in Prisons

Broderick Crawford cracked one of his teeth in California's Corcoran State Prison, where he was serving a sentence for attempted murder. Instead of going to the prison dentist, he decided to wait two years until he was released from prison to get dental care. He did not have any confidence in the prison dentist. "To put it bluntly," said California state senator Jackie Speier, "the health care system at CDC (California Department of Corrections) is sick. Twenty percent of the physicians that work at CDC have either a bad mark on their record or a series of malpractice lawsuits [from patients accusing them of poor medical care]—a figure that is four to five times higher than the general population of physicians in California."

However, doctors who work in the California correctional system disagree. They emphasize that the care they provide is just as good as the care patients receive in the communities from which the prisoners came. The prison doctors also point out that they face some obstacles that medical practitioners outside prisons do not have to deal with, such as often having to use outdated and inadequate equipment.

Many prisoners believe the medical care they receive is more than adequate. Clyde Hoffman, a prisoner in California, is one of them. In 2004, while receiving treatment for lung cancer, he said, "Everybody that works up here is excellent—this is far beyond my hopes and dreams that there'd be a place like this in prison."

Despite positive experiences such as Hoffman's, in 2006, the California prison health care system was ordered by federal judge Thelton Henderson to reform its operations. Henderson based his decision on years of personal observations and anecdotes he had heard from others. "I would tell politicians all the time," Henderson said, "Don't you understand there are people dying in prison every day because of diseases like asthma that are easily treatable? And they'd say that they understood but they had to be careful, because they couldn't be seen 'to hug a thug.'"

As a result of court-ordered reform efforts, more than sixty doctors were fired for incompetence, new physicians were hired, and corrections officers made a much greater effort to ensure that inmates got to their medical appointments. Prior to the reforms, one staff member estimated that 50 percent of patients did not make it to medical appointments because guards did not get them there on time. By 2015, correctional spending in California had increased, in part because of more spending on health care. However, these costs had been offset by reductions in the overall prison population. These reductions had been made because of problems with overcrowding.

Today, California spends more than any other state on health care for prisoners: $19,796 per person in 2015, up 25 percent from 2010, according to numbers released by the Pew Charitable Trusts in late 2017. The medium spending nationwide was $5,720 per inmate, for a total of $8.1 billion spent on prison health care in 2015.

Serving a Unique Population

The situation in California reflects a debate over prison health care that relates not only to the quality of care but also to its availability. Many people who are sent to correctional institutions suffer from chronic illnesses, such as heart ailments, diabetes, and asthma, or mental health problems. One of the reasons they have higher instances of health problems than the overall US population is that they tend to be members of lower income groups that have not been able to afford medical care in the past. Untreated mental health or substance-abuse problems might in turn make a person more likely to commit a crime.

As a result, the challenges that prison health care systems face are likely greater than those faced by medical care in the community outside prison walls. As Gary Maynard, president of the American Correctional Association, wrote in *Corrections Today*, "In many cases, correctional health care workers are treating inmates affected by life on the streets or in dangerous communities. They are treating intravenous drug users and the malnourished, both the underfed and those whose intake has little nutritional value. Many inmates never received childhood immunizations (for diseases like polio) and few have regular medical examinations."

According to *The Growth of Incarceration in the United States: Exploring Causes and Consequences*, a 2014 publication by the National Academies of Sciences, Engineering, and Medicine, inmates are ten to twenty times more likely to have a sexually transmitted disease. More than half of all prisoners have a mental health problem, and 68 percent have symptoms of drug or alcohol dependence or abuse, compared to 9 percent of the overall US population. More than 70 percent of prisoners who have a serious mental illness also have a substance-abuse problem. According to one study, as many as 39–43 percent of all prisoners have one or more chronic health conditions.

As it is in society at large, the cost of health care is among the fastest-growing category of prison operations. In addition to the overall increase in health care costs in the United States, another reason the cost of prison health care is rising is that more and more elderly prisoners are serving life sentence. Pew reports that older inmates are more likely to report having a chronic or past chronic condition and adds that, among women inmates, incidence of mental illness is significantly higher than average. The US Justice Department's inspector has found that, among federal prisons, those with the highest populations of aging prisoners spent, on average, five times more per inmate on health care and fourteen times more on medication.

Addressing Mental Health

Many prisons are doing their best to deal with the health care problems of inmates in their institutions. "Correctional health care is on the forefront of the battle against sexually transmitted diseases, including HIV/AIDS," writes Maynard. "The scope of mental health disorders for which treatment is available in institutions surpasses that available to indigents in the community, and prisons constitute the largest source of residential mental health treatment available in the country."

Nevertheless, mental health care in prisons is limited, writes Chris Koyanagi, policy director at the Bazelon Center for Mental Health Law, a nonprofit group that works on behalf of those with mental illness. "There's so much opportunity for prevention," he says. "But it seems we always want to wait, especially in mental health, until there's an emergency before we intervene." The Department of Justice has reported that about 25 percent of those inmates with mental illness are repeat offenders. Koyanagi points out that many such inmates have grown up without proper care, committed crimes, and returned to prison again and again. "You have all of these issues and then you get arrested. It's just one long trajectory of misery."

The number of mentally ill prisoners has increased dramatically over the past half century. There are numerous reasons for this, including cuts that have taken place in the number of community services offered to the mentally ill and cuts that have been made in the number of mental institutions. The number of mentally ill people living in institutions has shrank from 339 per 100,000 in 1955 to 29 per 100,000 in 1998. Many of those people who would have been in mental institutions fifty years ago are now in prisons instead.

Mental health problems are sometimes linked with substance abuse. Less than three in four state prisons offer treatment for drug and alcohol abuse or dependency, while almost every federal prison has such a program. Even so, just 40–50 percent of prisoners who abuse drugs actually participate in these programs.

Some argue that going to prison doesn't treat the underlying causes of criminal behavior for drug addicts, who may commit crimes such as theft to fund their habit. Instead, they insist, helping someone get over an addiction will be more effective in preventing such crimes in the future. Some states are even offering alternatives to prisons, programs called "drug courts," that put addicts on probation as they undergo treatment rather than sending them to jail or prison.

Sometimes individuals with mental health and substance-abuse problems are treated in the community and released, only to commit crimes and receive jail sentences. A study of women in this situation revealed that many were given medication in jail or at a mental health facility and released, with instructions to continue getting medical care in the community. However, these women, many of whom used crack cocaine, often did not continue treatment and were rearrested. Then they were given medication again. This happens both because it often is difficult to obtain medical care in the community at large and because those with mental health problems—once left to their own devices—often do not seek help or follow up on suggested treatment plans.

After repeatedly seeing the same women run through its system, the Sheriff's Office in Davidson County, Tennessee—the law-enforcement authority that oversees the county jail—tried a different approach. When asked why they used crack cocaine, many of the women had blamed mental illness. Then, when they were locked up, these same women had said that they used the legal medication they had received from doctors as a substitute for the crack they had used while on the street. Under the new approach, once in jail, such prisoners were forced to stop using crack and taken off any prescribed medications they were taking for various illnesses. Then they were watched closely and given medication only if severe problems occurred. In the end, "many of the women learned ... that they can cope well without legal or illegal drugs." Mental illness was not the key problem for this particular group of women; substance abuse had been the problem.

Elderly Prisoners

George Sanges, seventy-three years old and afflicted with cerebral palsy, was given a fifteen-year prison sentence after being convicted of assaulting his wife. Sanges was counted among those inmates fifty-five and older—a prison population that increased by 280 percent between 1999 and 2016. "With the elderly population, we're beginning to run something comparable to nursing homes," said Sharon Lewis, medical director for the Georgia Department of Corrections. "This is one of the unhealthiest populations found anywhere."

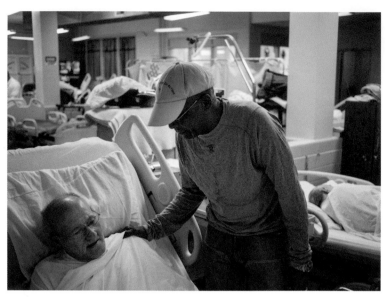

Donald Murray (*right*), 63, is one of the few inmates at the Louisiana State Penitentiary allowed to take care of other aging inmates.

While the population of elderly prisoners is increasing in part because those with longer sentences are getting older, the number of older prisoners being admitted into state prisons is actually on the rise. Four times as many aged fifty-five or older were admitted in 2013 than in 1993, according to the Bureau of Justice Statistics.

Several states have prisons set aside for older inmates, sometimes defined as those above the age of fifty and other times defined as those fifty-five or older. For instance, the Allen-Oakwood Correctional Facility in Ohio established a special unit for prisoners over the age of fifty to treat those with physical illnesses and those suffering from dementia-related problems. Experts point out that prisons need health care workers with special training to deal with elderly prisoners. They must be able to spot those who are beginning to suffer from senility or depression or those who might be considering suicide. These problems are more common among older prisoners than the rest of the inmate population. Older patients also do better in less-crowded prisons, with daily exercise programs and chances to interact with other prisoners.

While many in American society feel sympathy upon hearing about the rough life that sick and elderly prisoners often have to deal with, others do not. Foremost among them are the families of the victims. "Why should they be in a nursing home where their family gets to come and comfort them and say goodbye to them at their death bed? I can't say goodbye to my loved one," Shawn Chambers-Galis of Pennsylvania told the *Philadelphia Daily News* in 2006, in response to a story the newspaper was doing on a bill that would grant "compassionate release" to terminally ill inmates. "[An early release is] not what my justice system assured me would happen. I will agree with this the day they show me my brother's appeal process to get out of his grave." Chambers-Galis's brother and another man were shot and killed by an acquaintance in Alaska.

Education in Prison

Many prison inmates lack even the high school education that might have enabled them to find steady employment before being incarcerated. Prior to 1965, few prisons provided any educational opportunities for prisoners. The riot at Attica Prison in 1971, followed by prison reform, changed that situation. Correctional facilities offered prisoners courses that enabled them to obtain high school equivalency diplomas. Meanwhile, Congress had also enacted a new law that offered prisoners financial aid if they took college courses. According to Marlene Martin, national director of the Campaign to End the Death Penalty, "it was enough to sustain college education programs in 90 percent of states."

Inmates at San Quentin State Prison in California learn computer coding in 2016 so they can get good jobs once they're released.

Then, in 1994, Congress passed new legislation, the Violent Crime Control and Law Enforcement Act, which cut off these grants. The reasoning for this was simple: people wanted to know why prisoners should get free education when those who are not jailed are required to pay for it. The act's passage had an instant impact behind bars. "Immediately programs began to shut down," wrote Martin. This was part of an effort, added Martin, "in a more conservative direction ... The idea that it should be a concern of society to help prisoners better themselves disappeared; instead, prison became a place where people were thrown away to pay for their crimes."

In 2007, Congress changed direction once again and passed the Second Chance Act, which has since given out more than eight hundred grants in forty-nine states. This law provides funding for new education programs in prisons and was enacted to help improve recidivism rates. Over the past two decades, studies have shown that inmates who improve their education while in prison are less likely to be rearrested. In one study of more than three thousand inmates in Maryland, Ohio, and Minnesota, only 21 percent of those who participated in education programs were incarcerated again, compared to 31 percent who did not enroll in these programs.

"Those who participate in higher education in prison are less likely to go back and less likely to fail in the workplace," explains Max Kenner, founder and executive director of the Bard Prison Initiative in New York. They realize that an education gives them a better chance to support themselves in the community and stay out of prison.

According to another study conducted in 2007, even completion of a high school program can help inmates find jobs once they are released. Not only do inmates improve their skills, but they also show potential employers that they are serious about making an effort to find a steady job.

During the first decade of the twenty-first century, many states offered high school diploma programs or general education development certificate programs, in addition to higher education, to inmates. In North Carolina, the state Department of Correction and the North Carolina Community College system worked together to enable about one-third of all inmates to take college courses annually. They could even finish their degrees once they were released from prison by utilizing partnership opportunities offered by community colleges and universities. Boston University's Prison Education Program offers the chance to earn a bachelor's degree or certificate in interdisciplinary studies. Since the program was founded, hundreds of participants have received their degrees. The program also includes mentoring for individual students after their release from prison. Lanny Kutakoff, former director of the program, said, "We discovered [that] having this kind of relationship profoundly impacts students' grades and retention rates."

Today, high school classes are offered in 84 percent of state prisons; just 27 percent offer college classes. Vocational training—classes to learn the skills for a particular profession—is offered in almost all federal prisons, but just 44 percent of private prisons and 7 percent of jails have vocational classes.

Chapter Four

VIOLENCE BEHIND BARS

"**I**nmates have weapons," said Frank Shaw, warden of the East Mississippi Correctional Facility, as he sat on the witness stand. "It's a fact of life." Shaw was testifying in a civil rights lawsuit, filed by the Southern Poverty Law Center and the American Civil Liberties Union, which alleged dangerous conditions and understaffing at the privately run facility where Shaw worked.

An expert witness and former Washington State prisons chief, Eldon Vail confirmed that prisoners in the facility indeed had weapons and offered his theory as to why. Because there were so few guards in the prison, he said, inmates made weapons to protect themselves. Meanwhile, a shortage of medical staff led to

Opposite: Some inmates were injured after a disturbance involving eighty prisoners at the Men's Central Jail in Los Angeles in 2015. Paramedics and police responded to the incident, as seen in this video still.

situations in which prisoners with mental illnesses were acting out more often, more violently. Indeed, photos and surveillance offered as evidence showed fire damage to a cell door, excessive blood spilled in a corner, and a violent assault to which it took nearly half an hour for guards to respond.

Nearly one in five male prisoners say that other inmates have physically assaulted them, and 21 percent alleged they've been attacked by prison staff, *Mother Jones* reports. What's more, 22 percent report that they have been sexually assaulted by another inmate; 33 percent by staff members.

One of the most pressing issues for people calling for prison reform is the level of violence in US prisons. Learning about these horrors—and just how widespread they seem to be—is necessary for gaining a deeper understanding of the debate around the future of prisons in the United States.

Victims and the Obstacles They Face

Both men and women can be victims of sexual assault in prisons. The experience is traumatizing for these victims. In a 2009 report by the National Prison Rape Elimination Commission, former inmate Necole Brown revealed in an interview, "I continue to contend with flashbacks of what this correctional officer did to me and the guilt, shame, and rage that comes with having been sexually violated for so many years." Tom Cahill, who spent only one night in a jail in San Antonio, Texas, reported that after being sexually assaulted by a group of men, "I've been hospitalized more times than I can count and I didn't pay for those hospitalizations, the taxpayers paid. My career as a journalist and photographer was completely derailed."

Particularly at risk are lesbian, gay, bisexual, transgender, and queer (LGBTQ) inmates, who are sexually abused ten times more than those prisoners who identify as heterosexual, according to the Bureau of Justice Statistics. One gay inmate, Rodney Smith—who used a pseudonym for his own protection as he talked to nonprofit social justice publication *Rewire.News*—reported that he was constantly assaulted by multiple people under threat of violence for a period of eight months. He was afraid to report the assaults for fear of being violently attacked.

Overcrowding and lack of staff have made protection for prisoners far more difficult. Many prisoners are, like Smith, unwilling or unable to report sexual abuse. They fear being bullied or harmed if they speak out," reported the National Prison Rape Elimination Commission. They also believe that some members of the staff will not pay attention to them. Inmate Cyryna Pasion told the commissioners, "When I told one of the guards I trusted how tired I was of putting up with abuse, he told me to just ignore it."

Many staff are still untrained in conducting investigations of sexual abuse, and only a small number of those accused of abuse are prosecuted. In addition, the victims frequently do not receive counseling after an incident, nor do they receive HIV testing. Michael Blucker entered a correctional center in Illinois with no indication of HIV, but a year after his incarceration and after being victimized by rape, he had contracted the disease.

Catalysts to Violence

Inmates earn small amounts of money—sometimes as little as twelve cents an hour—for the work that they are assigned to do in prison. They use their wages to buy items from the prison store and also to pay restitution to those they have committed crimes against, if they have been ruled to do so.

However, with little money available to them, and especially if no one from outside the prison is sending them money, they often borrow from other inmates and go into debt. This makes them vulnerable to pressure that may lead to physical violence if the debts are not repaid. Some try to earn money by making themselves available to staff members for sexual favors. Marianne McNabb, a private criminal justice consultant to various private and state agencies, suggests that correctional facilities provide better training for staff members regarding policies prohibiting sexual violence. One way to do this might be to frequently remind staff members of prison policies regarding the exploitation of inmates. In addition, prisoners should be given reassurance that if they report incidents, something will be done about them.

McNabb reports many women prisoners, beginning at a young age, have experienced victimization, violence, and trauma, including both physical and sexual trauma. Many women inmates also have a history of substance abuse, poor family relationships, and economic hardship. As a result, inmates may come to rely on other inmates as part of an extended family. Therefore, prison staff must ensure that, as much as possible, these relationships are not abusive. If incidents do occur, women need to receive counseling from professionals who understand the needs of female inmates. "The good news is that safety for women in jails and prisons has improved," McNabb concludes. "The response to the Prison Rape Elimination Act on the part of correctional administrators and policy makers has meant a serious realignment of priorities and resources." She adds that policies and sanctions regarding staff sexual misconduct have reportedly curtailed the most obvious cases of such behavior.

Corrections Officers

Many corrections officers fear they will become targets of violence committed by prisoners. The numbers support their fear. In 1995, one report submitted to the Department of Justice said there were more than fourteen thousand reported attacks on corrections officers by inmates, using weapons such as broken glass, safety razors, and sharpened toothbrushes. The assaults led to the death of fourteen staff members. Just five years later, there were roughly eighteen thousand attacks on corrections officers.

The job of a correctional officer has become more difficult as inmate populations have increased. Thus, additional training has become necessary. Theodis Beck, former secretary of the North Carolina Department of Correction, explained, "Today's correctional officer must be able to look at situations from an inmate's perspective. He must be in tune to the changing situation of aging inmates, know how to deal with offenders who may be suicidal, be able to recognize gang signs and colors, speak foreign languages, and be sensitive to issues involving supervision of offenders of the opposite sex."

For example, gangs may flourish inside a correctional facility. In 2005, a gang inside the Bayside Correctional Facility in New Jersey initiated a violent uprising that injured twenty-nine correctional officers before it was finally brought under control. Officers later testified before New Jersey's Assembly Prison Gang Violence Task Force that they had received little or no training in "how to identify gang members, what their gang signs and nicknames are, how they move and with whom they associate." Officers also did not know how to deal with a major threat inside a prison. The task force recommended that all staff should receive at least sixteen hours of gang training and also learn how to handle riots as well as how to stop the flow of all types of contraband. Officers also needed to be made aware of information about gangs that was being collected by the Department of Corrections' Special Investigations Division, which provides assistance with intelligence and investigations to law enforcement agencies of all levels.

A correctional officer's job can be extremely stressful. In some prisons, a single officer is responsible for supervising as

A Different Kind of Correctional Facility

Corrections officer Lou West works in a pod, part of the design of a direct-supervision correctional facility. These institutions began to appear in the 1970s in New York City, San Diego, and Chicago as part of the federal prison system. They differed from the traditional prison design that consisted of cells along long hallways that were patrolled periodically by correctional officers. As authors Christine Tartaro and Marissa Levy wrote in *American Jails* magazine, "An obvious problem with intermittent supervision is that inmates have until the officer's next patrol to assault cellmates or commit other types of infractions."

In a direct-supervision facility, cells are built around a dayroom where inmates have recreational activities, educational programs, and meals. A ratio of one officer to about sixty prisoners is common, and

At the Cayuga County Jail in New York, there were four direct-supervision pods in 2006, one of which is pictured here.

the correctional officer interacts with the prisoners directly. Each pod is relatively independent, and officers provide services to the inmates in their pod. If an officer spots a problem with an inmate or recognizes that a conflict may be about to occur between inmates, he or she is expected to step in and diffuse the situation. After daily activities are completed, the prisoners return to their cells, which can be easily observed by an officer in the dayroom.

"In the pod, there's no getting away from the inmates," Officer West told the Commission on Safety and Abuse in America's Prisons. "I'm asked to address all their needs and to be ready for any emotional disturbance." West is in charge of sixty-seven inmates.

Studies suggest various benefits to the direct-supervision approach. Relations between officers and inmates are more positive because they interact more often. There is also less violence among inmates and against correctional staff members.

To be successful in a direct-supervision facility, officers need to receive training in communications skills and interpersonal relationships, especially for cases in which they need to diffuse a potentially violent situation. Yet many facilities provide an average of only two days' training in communication to their officers. In addition, overcrowding can make an officer's job far more difficult.

many as one hundred inmates, many of whom may be violent. They may threaten a correctional officer at any time. Weapons are presumably unavailable to inmates; nevertheless, some gain possession of them. They may fashion a safety razor into a weapon, file down a toothbrush until it becomes dangerous, or attach a blade to the end of a toothbrush.

In 2009, *American Jails* cited a study that said, "Attacks on property or persons within the facility are common because inmates are bored and frustrated, and they may threaten, or become verbally/physically assaultive to other inmates and staff … [I]nmates use violence as a way to feel self-important due to interpersonal failures." Prisons often do not provide sufficient counseling and educational programs to deal with these issues. In addition, officers' stress may arise from sources outside their job sites. Some studies have pointed out that since correctional officers are often portrayed as brutes in the news and in popular media, they sometimes distance themselves from those close to them on a personal level, such as family.

The effects of stress vary among correctional staff. As is the case in many other occupations, some staff members suffer from high blood pressure and heart disease, while others develop anger-management problems and take out their anger on inmates or family members. Still others suffer from drug-abuse problems.

Problems exist in all correctional systems, including federal ones. On June 20, 2008, for example, Corrections officer Jose Rivera was stabbed to death by two prisoners at the US Penitentiary in Atwater, California. The federal system, which includes Atwater, was short-staffed during that time period, and inmate crowding had raised the prison population to 37 percent above capacity. At the same time, violence against corrections officers had increased, up 6 percent from 2005. This suggested that there may be a relationship between overcrowding and violence.

Testifying in front of the US House of Representatives, Bryan Lowry, then president of the American Federation of Government Employees' Council of Prison Locals, pointed out, "High security penitentiaries currently assign only one correctional officer to each housing unit. This unsound correctional practice is particularly dangerous during the evening watch shift when only one officer is available to perform the 4:00 p.m. inmate count and the 11:00 p.m. inmate lockup." Correctional officer Rivera was alone, locking inmates into the cells for the 4 p.m. inmate count, when he was murdered. In 2008, the Bureau of Prisons assigned another staff member to high-security facilities for the evening shifts. In addition, the Bureau of Prisons decided to make available to all correctional officers protective vests that enable officers to resist stab wounds.

Lowry also called on the Bureau of Prisons to step up its inmate work program. Congress had cut funding to this program during the first decade of the twenty-first century as a cost-savings measure. Nevertheless, studies have shown that the program helped prevent boredom among the prisoners and the violence that could result from it. The program also instilled work values

Inmates build a dog house as part of a Construction Technologies class at the Shawnee Correctional Center in Illinois in 2018.

and enabled prisoners to learn important skills. Those who were employed by the program were also 35 percent less likely to return to prison during the first twelve months after their release because many of them could find jobs in the community. All of these measures have the potential to reduce stress for correctional officers and improve their safety as they work in prisons.

By no means are inmates the only ones guilty of committing violence behind bars. Often, corrections officers are charged with abuse. In June 2010, for example, a former corrections officer at California's Chino State Prison was sentenced to more than four years in prison for abusing inmates in a 2002 incident. He had thrown shackled inmates to the ground and conspired to cover it up. Similar claims of abuse—frequently of a sexual nature—turn up in newspaper headlines on a regular basis.

Legislating Prison Violence

The Prison Rape Elimination Act (PREA) of 2003 set a "zero-tolerance standard" for rape and ordered the Department of Justice to "make the prevention of prison rape a top priority in each prison system." States that fail to comply could see their federal funding slashed.

Since that time, there has been progress in dealing with sexual violence in prison. The National Institute of Corrections has conducted workshops for correctional officers, and training programs have been instituted at prisons across the United States. Ohio is one state that has adopted such a program, and correctional administrators there have reported an "overall change in tone" as a result.

A majority of states have staff training programs, as well as periodic refresher courses to review the training principles. Corrections officers learn how to detect possible perpetrators of sexual violence, both inmates and staff members; how to identify possible victims; and how to conduct incident investigations, protect the safety of inmates under their care, and discipline those who are guilty of sexual violence.

In addition, states offer educational programs to inmates regarding sexual violence when they are processed at selection centers. These include information about the Prison Rape Elimination Act, their rights as victims, how to report incidents, and how to prevent rape by another inmate or member of the staff.

Nevertheless, a 2006 study of the Texas prison system revealed that incidents of rape continued. Indeed, Texas had the highest rate in the United States. The study showed that a majority of victims were younger than their attackers and suffering from mental health problems. Potential victims were supposed to be identified in the state screening process during intake and offered protection. Overcrowding and a reduced officer-to-inmate ratio had made this impossible in many cases.

In 2016, a provision was added to PREA that allowed for states to stop reporting their progress in complying with the law in 2022. This means that states will no longer face the same consequences—in the form of small cuts in funding—that came with failure to follow the rules of PREA.

Chapter Five

JUVENILES IN THE PRISON SYSTEM

Photographer Richard Ross has visited juvenile detention centers throughout the United States, taking photos of the inmates and learning their stories. Much of what he's seen or heard in these centers still haunts him. He recalls, for instance, a fifth-grader who had been taken to a Reno, Nevada, center because he had acted up at school. His single mother wouldn't be able to pick him up for several more hours.

"He was drinking warm milk, like someone gave him a cardboard thing of milk. I can still smell that milk. That intake area smelled like elementary school," Ross remembered.

However, many of the inmates Ross met weren't going to be released any time soon. They came from

Opposite: A juvenile is shown in shackles. On any given day in the United States, more than fifty thousand juveniles are being held in criminal-justice facilities.

homes where their parents, if they were present at all, abused drugs or alcohol, or even assaulted them. Some of the juveniles had abused drugs themselves, following in their parents' footsteps. Others suffered from crippling depression. Ross recalls one girl who told him over and over, "I can't wait to get out of here so I can kill myself."

On any given day, according to the Prison Policy Initiative, almost 53,000 juveniles are being held in juvenile criminal-justice-related facilities. Juvenile detention centers are similar to jails and prisons. While juveniles are often lodged separately from adults, they can still be tried as adults at a court's discretion, and nearly one in ten are in adult prisons or jails. Nearly nine in ten are in locked facilities, and two in three are held for periods longer than a month. Whether this type of detention is necessary or appropriate for individuals who are not yet adults remains a matter of heated debate.

Who Are These Juvenile Inmates?

About 16,000 of those in detention centers are being detained until a judge can hear their case or hand down their sentencing. Almost one in four are being held for minor offenses such as truancy or not completing community service, the Prison Policy Institute reports. Nationally, about 15 percent of juveniles in detention facilities are females.

African American youths and people of color comprise a disproportionate number of those in correctional facilities. The Prison Policy Institute outlines some striking statistics: "While less than 14% of all youth under 18 in the U.S. are Black, 43% of boys and 34% of girls in juvenile facilities are Black. And even excluding youth held in Indian country facilities, American

Indians make up 3% of girls and 1.5% of boys in juvenile facilities, despite comprising less than 1% of all youth nationally."

Many reports have been issued in an attempt to determine the reasons for such glaring racial discrepancies. One prepared in 2009 by the Criminal Justice Program of the National Conference of State Legislatures said those explanations range from "jurisdictional issues, certain police practices and punitive juvenile crime legislation of the 1990s to perceived racial bias in the system." The report offered further explanation on each of these four topics:

Jurisdictional issues: Cases tried in urban areas, where minority populations are concentrated, are more likely to result in harsher outcomes than similar cases in nonurban areas where more whites are located. Also, urban crimes tend to be more visible to law enforcement than nonurban ones.

Certain police practices: Many police practices target low-income urban neighborhoods where minorities live.

Punitive juvenile laws: Tough laws that have made it easier to try youths as adults for certain crimes have disproportionately impacted minority youths.

Perceived racial bias: Several studies conducted by the Office of Juvenile Justice and Delinquency Prevention have shown that bias against people of color was present at various stages of the criminal justice system.

Juvenile Courts

During the early part of the nineteenth century, youths accused of crime were treated just like adults. They were given harsh sentences, locked away in adult prisons, and sometimes even hanged for their crimes. However, by the middle part of the nineteenth century changes were underway as reformers led a successful effort to treat children differently from adults. They persuaded political leaders that many youths accused of crimes had come from impoverished homes and turned to robbery or some other form of crime as a way to survive. Detention centers, called reform schools, that were dedicated to house only juvenile offenders soon opened. These schools were designed to reform delinquent youths, train them in vocational skills, and eventually return them to the community after completion of their sentence.

In 1899, Chicago became the first city to begin a juvenile justice system. By 1925, almost every state had a juvenile court system. In juvenile court, the rules were quite different from the adult court system. There were no juries; instead, judges heard the cases brought against juveniles and made a decision. In juvenile court, a youth was never considered guilty of a crime; instead, he or she was "adjudicated delinquent." Many of these youths were returned to the community on probation and under the authority of a probation officer. Others were sent to reform schools to serve out their sentences.

Problems soon arose in these institutions, however. Younger delinquents sometimes fell prey to older youths who physically and sexually abused them. For these and other reasons, reform schools proved to be an ineffective way to rehabilitate youths, and many children remained in institutions for long sentences. So, by the end of the twentieth century, the courts were making every effort to keep juveniles out of reform schools and place them back in the community instead. For instance, they might be sent to group homes or shelters—residential homes where people who share common characteristics live—where they were carefully monitored by shelter staff as well as probation officers.

Beginning in the 1960s, Congress passed a series of laws designed to more effectively safeguard the rights of juveniles in the justice system. Under the Juvenile Justice and Delinquency Prevention Act (JJDPA) of 1974, Congress ordered that any juveniles who had committed "status offenses"—which were

Fifteen-year-old Austin Hancock (*center*) pleads guilty to four counts of attempted murder and one count of inducing panic in an Ohio court.

generally quite minor—should not be placed in correctional facilities. In 1980, Congress amended the act, stating that juveniles could not be placed in the same cells as adults while awaiting appearances in court.

When a case is referred to juvenile court, it is evaluated by an intake officer or a prosecutor, depending on the way the particular court is structured. The officer or prosecutor looks at the evidence and decides whether the case should proceed. Some cases are dismissed due to lack of evidence. About half the cases are "handled informally," as stated in the *Juvenile Offenders and Victims: 2006 National Report*. In many of these cases, juveniles who have admitted their guilt agree to perform certain types of activities under an agreement known as a consent decree. These activities may include drug counseling or community service. If the juvenile carries out these responsibilities, the case will be dismissed.

Other cases proceed to court, where the juvenile's lawyer and the lawyer prosecuting the case argue its merits in front of a judge. Witnesses appear to testify in the case, and then the judge considers the evidence and makes a final decision. During the proceedings, the juvenile may be required to remain in a detention center. In the final decision, many defendants are ordered to serve probation, a supervision program in which the offender must complete certain requirements such as meeting a curfew or attending certain programs. In addition, they may be required to have counseling and even to report to a detention center on weekends. In roughly 25 percent of the cases, the juvenile is ordered by the judge to confinement in a juvenile detention center for a specific prison term. These cases involve serious offenses such as murder, rape, and robbery.

Juvenile Detention Facilities

The National Center for Juvenile Justice reports that, in 2016, 71 percent of juvenile offenders were held in public facilities versus 29 percent in private. These facilities self-classified in a number of different categories: 38 percent as residential treatment centers; 37 percent as detention centers; 19 percent as group homes; 11 percent as long-term secure facilities; 7 percent as shelters; 3 percent as reception/diagnostic centers; and 2 percent as ranch/wilderness camps. Eighty percent reported being under capacity, while 15 percent were at capacity and 4 percent were over capacity.

A 2014 report found that "mechanical restraints" such as restraining chairs, leg cuffs, and handcuffs, were used in 62 percent of long-term secure facilities and 43 percent of detention centers.

Juvenile detention facilities vary in terms of the conditions in which juveniles are confined. In "locked" facilities, youths are locked in their rooms at night for sleeping, or they may be sent to locked rooms when they cause a disturbance. In addition, these facilities often have security fences around them and locked gates. The Prison Policy Institute reports that 89 percent of youths who are in some sort of juvenile detention are in locked facilities.

Other facilities are "staff secure." That is, staff members provide security instead of using locks to confine juveniles. These

Key Supreme Court Decisions

The US Supreme Court has made several rulings that had an important impact on the rights of juveniles. One of these rulings involved the case of twelve-year-old Samuel Winship, who was accused of stealing $112 from a woman's handbag. Winship was adjudicated delinquent based on the "preponderance of the evidence." This was standard in juvenile courts at the time, rather than "proof beyond a reasonable doubt," which was required under the US Constitution for adult defendants. In 1970, the Supreme Court ruled that juvenile courts should use the same, higher standard of "proof beyond a reasonable doubt" for juveniles.

In a vast majority of jurisdictions, juvenile courts do not have jury trials. That leaves decisions up to the judge based on the evidence presented in a case. When sixteen-year-old Joseph McKeiver was accused of robbery and larceny in 1968, his lawyer asked for a jury trial. The request was denied. McKeiver's lawyers appealed, and the case reached the Supreme Court. In *McKeiver v. Pennsylvania* (1971), the Supreme Court ruled that a jury was unnecessary in juvenile courts.

In 1977, Gregory Martin, then fourteen, was charged with robbery and assault, and held in detention. When a youth is accused of a serious crime, he may be held in detention pending his appearance in court if he is considered a "serious risk" to the community. Martin's lawyer challenged this detention, stating that it was a violation of a fundamental right under the US Constitution, that a defendant cannot be punished without a trial. Detention, the lawyer argued, was punishment. In *Schall v. Martin* (1984), the US Supreme Court disagreed, explaining that preventive detention serves to protect both the juvenile and society.

In more recent cases, the Supreme Court has ruled that neither the death penalty nor life sentences may be levied against juveniles.

facilities generally serve youths judged delinquent for less serious crimes, such as minor drug and alcohol violations. Staff-secure facilities include wilderness camps, group homes, and boot camps.

Most juveniles in residential facilities are age twelve and older. In Wisconsin, for example, youths twelve and older can be placed in secured juvenile correctional institutions. Those who have committed serious crimes may receive sentences of five years or more. If that sentence lasts past the offender's eighteenth birthday, he or she can be transferred to an adult facility. During a brief orientation, staff members talk to juveniles, explain the rules, and provide them with any other information they need. They are screened by a staff that includes social workers, youth counselors, and mental health experts. For example, when juveniles enter a detention facility in Wisconsin, they are routinely tested to determine whether they have problems with drugs or alcohol, or whether they require mental health counseling. In that state, any juveniles who have not yet graduated from high school are required to attend school at the facility. A variety of mandatory treatment programs also are available, including drug and alcohol counseling, anger management, vocational training, and computer courses. Other states offer similar programs.

Challenges and Obstacles

Despite efforts by Wisconsin and other states to reform and rehabilitate juvenile delinquents, many problems have been reported in detention facilities. In 2008, Mississippi decided to close the Columbia Training School, a facility for juveniles, many of whom were runaways from abusive homes. The staff allegedly had abused juvenile inmates. Ashley Fantz, a reporter for CNN, interviewed an inmate named Erica, who said she had been chained and handcuffed when she had meals or went to the bathroom. Fantz also quoted a note written by a fifteen-year-old girl who alleged she had been sexually abused by a facility staff

A juvenile inmate at a Tucson, Arizona, youth detention facility waits to eat his lunch.

member. Meanwhile, in Florida, there have been at least seven deaths among juvenile inmates since 2000. Texas has fired or disciplined at least ninety staff members during the same period for sexual abuse.

Another report by the Justice Department stated that more than four thousand juveniles in correctional facilities, or about seventeen per one thousand, were sexually abused by staff members or other inmates between 2005 and 2006. Inmates who abuse or attack other inmates are often admired by the rest of the juvenile prisoners, according to the report.

According to the "National Prison Rape Elimination Commission Report" of 2009, "Juveniles in confinement are much more likely than incarcerated adults to be sexually abused." Bureau of Justice Statistics data from 2014 indicates that 9.5 percent of youth in juvenile detention and 1.8 in adult facilities are sexually assaulted. In one example, in a juvenile facility in Indiana, youths as young as twelve years old were sexually abused by older teenagers. Children weighing as little as 70 pounds (32 kilograms) were being abused by those outweighing them by 100 pounds (45 kg) or more. The smaller kids had little chance of fending off the older inmates.

There have also been reports of problems in boot camps for juvenile delinquents. These are programs that often take place in wilderness areas where youths are required to submit to strict military discipline during their sentence in an attempt to reform their behavior. As reported by the Government Accountability Office, a watchdog agency of the federal government, these programs serve between ten thousand and twenty thousand youths at a cost of about $130 to $450 per day—money that ultimately comes from taxpayers.

Over the years, the Government Accountability Office has investigated several deaths of youths who were placed in these programs. At least thirty-five juveniles have died in boot camps since 1983, and others have suffered broken bones. One of these was sixteen-year-old Aaron Bacon, who had been sent to boot camp in 1994 after he was found to be using drugs in school. According to Aaron's father, Bob, the teen spent fourteen days with little food and was required to take daily hikes of about 8 to 10 miles (12.8 to 16 kilometers). Bob Bacon said, "On the days he did have food, it consisted of undercooked lentils, lizards, scorpions, trail mix and a celebrated canned peach on the thirteenth day." Aaron Bacon died while at boot camp.

In 2008, reporter Seamus McGraw wrote about fourteen-year-old Tony Haynes, who been sent to boot camp after being arrested for shoplifting. Haynes, according to witnesses, wanted to leave the program and was punished for this by being forced to sit outside in temperatures that reached 110°F (43°C), with no water. Soon afterward, he died.

Other young people, however, have found the camps beneficial. Pedro Madrid, according to his mother, changed his entire life as a result of an experience at boot camp.

A study of New York juvenile detention released in 2009 by the US Department of Justice revealed that "Excessive physical force was routinely used to discipline children at several juvenile prisons … resulting in broken bones, shattered teeth, concussions and dozens of other serious injuries." The report added, "Anything from sneaking an extra cookie to initiating a fist fight may result in a full prone restraint with handcuffs. This one-size-fits-all approach has, not surprisingly, led to an alarming number of serious injuries to youth[s]." The report went on to point out that force violated the inmates' constitutional rights against "cruel and unusual punishment."

Youths in Adult Detention

During the past few decades, public opinion has supported harsher punishment for juveniles who are guilty of very serious crimes. In thirteen states, there is no minimum age for transferring a juvenile to criminal court and trying him or her as an adult. Some states have minimum ages set at ten, twelve, or thirteen years old. In fact, children as young as eight years old have been tried as adults, according to the Equal Justice Initiative, an organization that aims to end mass incarceration in the United States.

In the United States, an estimated two hundred thousand juveniles and children are tried as adult each year, according to a 2018 report from the Inter-American Commission on Human Rights. The majority of states allow these juveniles to be housed in adult facilities. Although the Juvenile Justice and Delinquency Prevention Act requires that juveniles and adults be housed separately, this doesn't apply to those who are tried as adults. These youths in adult facilities are five times more likely to be subjected to sexual assault than if they were held in juvenile facilities.

An increasing number of juveniles have also been sentenced to life in prison without parole for crimes such as murder. "Criminal punishment in the United States can serve four goals," states Human Rights Watch, a leading human rights organization, "rehabilitation, retribution, deterrence and incapacitation … Sentencing children to life without parole fails to measure up on all counts." Many such prisoners were less than sixteen years

In the Orange County Juvenile Hall mental health unit in 2013, Mike Roman (*center*) teaches a class for juvenile inmates.

old when they were sentenced. While many were murderers, others had been "participants in a robbery or burglary in which a murder was committed by someone else." Only thirteen other nations in the world impose such life sentences on juveniles.

However, many people believe that the old adage "an eye for an eye" should apply to all criminals, regardless of age. In 2009, New York State representative William Snyder told the *New York Times* why he believes this should be the case. "Sometimes a 15-year-old has a tremendous appreciation for right and wrong," he said. "I think it would be wrong for the Supreme Court to say that it was patently illegal or improper to send a youthful offender to life without parole. At a certain point, juveniles cross the line, and they have to be treated as adults and punished as adults."

Nevertheless, states throughout the country are currently examining their juvenile facilities and urging improvements. In 2009, Washington, DC, closed Oak Hill, "considered one of the worst juvenile detention facilities in the country," Eileen Rivers reports in *USA TODAY*. In its place, the city developed a program that prioritizes keeping kids in the community and offers a wealth of education options. An estimated 65 percent of juveniles in the program serve their detention in the community, rather than in locked facilities. For its part, Berks County, Pennsylvania, established an evening reporting center in an area of high juvenile crime. This is an alternative to detention while juveniles are waiting for court appearances. The center provides counseling, help with homework, recreation, and more.

Juveniles and Mental Health

As a result of the 2007–2009 economic recession, many states reduced their expenditures for mental health counseling in towns, cities, and schools. Instead, states relied more heavily on juvenile detention centers to deal with young people whose mental health problems may have resulted in criminal activities. "We're seeing more and more mentally ill kids who couldn't find community programs that were intensive enough to treat them," said Joseph Penn, director of mental health services for the University of Texas Medical Branch Correctional Managed Care at the time. "Jails and juvenile justice facilities are the new asylums."

The situation was especially serious in California. In Los Angeles County, for example, Dr. Eric Trupin, a psychologist and consultant for the correctional system, pointed out that "some detainees appeared to be held there for no reason other than that they were mentally ill and the county had no other institution capable of treating them."

The mental health staff members who try to help juvenile inmates may have very little information about them. Many of the inmates come from families that are not intact, and school records may not accompany an inmate to a correctional facility.

The National Alliance on Mental Illness estimates that as many as 70 percent of juveniles and children arrested each year in the United States have a mental health condition. Imprisonment and especially solitary confinement can make such conditions worse, NAMI reports.

Chapter Six

DETAINING IMMIGRANTS

When twelve-year-old Leticia and her ten-year-old brother, Walter, were separated from their mother and placed in a detention facility in southern Texas in May 2018, all they had was each other. They were forced to wash the bathrooms, follow strict lights-out curfews, and line up for food. They weren't allowed to sit on the floor, and crying was discouraged. Even when Leticia wanted to comfort her brother with a hug, "they told me I couldn't touch him," she remembers.

Leticia and Walter were among the thousands of immigrant children, some as young as two years old, who had been subject to a new US policy in which any families caught crossing the US border illegally

Opposite: A two-year-old girl, daughter of an asylum seeker from Honduras, cries while her mother is detained and searched at the United States–Mexico border on June 12, 2018.

were separated. Most weren't able to maintain contact with their parents, who were being detained and prosecuted elsewhere. The no-hugging policy was widespread in these detention centers, and according to a number of experts, it increased the stress that these children were already suffering and risked inflicting both short-term and long-term health problems and trauma on them.

As a result of a new "zero-tolerance" Trump administration policy on illegal immigration, more than 2,654 children were separated from their parents, according to the US Government Accountability Office. The number of children at shelters for migrants increased fivefold between May 2017 and September 2018 to 12,800, according to the *New York Times*; many of these children had been unaccompanied across the border. At the same time, fewer children were being released from detention facilities to live with sponsors or foster families. Former First Lady Laura Bush called such facilities "eerily reminiscent" of the internment camps used to house Japanese Americans during World War II. These camps targeted people solely because of their race.

Audio recordings and photos of crying children spread like wildfire through the news and social media, and much of the country was outraged. At first, the administration held fast to its policy. "If people don't want to be separated from their children, they should not bring them with them," insisted then attorney general Jeff Sessions. Nevertheless, facing mounting public pressure, Trump moved to change the policy in June 2018.

The US government began to slowly reunite families. However, many of the children's and parents' information had not been correctly documented, and by September, 437 children still remained in the custody of the Office of Refugee Resettlement. Some of their parents had been deported, while others had been deemed unfit. By October, sixty-six children were still not reunited with their families. That same month, it was confirmed that the administration had failed to realize that fourteen children were in government care. According to the *San Francisco Chronicle*, a recent report found that "officials feel no obligation to find children who were released to other homes before a judge ordered an accounting of them, suggesting the total separated under the policy may never be known."

By October 2018, the Trump administration was again considering a policy in which parents and children would be separated at the border, the *Washington Post* reports.

What should the policy around detaining undocumented immigrants be? Should immigration officials take a more compassionate approach to families, or should everyone who has broken the law by entering the country without permission be treated the same? Are parents who bring their children across the border irresponsible or simply doing everything they can to achieve a better life for their families? All of these questions have sparked heated debates in the area of immigration detention for years—perhaps never more so than with the family-separation controversy of 2018.

Housing Immigrant Families

The T. Don Hutto Residential Center in Taylor, Texas, was, until 2009, one of two immigrant detention facilities in the United States that housed families. Hutto, as it is called, is run by the Corrections Corporation of America, a prison management company started in 1983. It is one of several private companies that run prisons used by the Department of Homeland Security to house immigrants.

Some of these immigrants have entered the United States illegally; others who seek asylum are being held while their cases are being heard; still others are incarcerated for committing crimes. Since many immigrants have children, Congress decided that if parents were held in custody, their children could not be left without anywhere to live. So the Department of Homeland Security—as reported by Margaret Talbot, a *New Yorker* writer who did an in-depth piece in 2008 on children housed in immigrant detention facilities—decided to incarcerate them in facilities like Hutto.

Talbot's article relates the plight of several families, including that of Salwan Komo, his wife, Neven, and their infant daughter. The Komos were refugees from Iraq who came to the United States seeking asylum, or protection, from Muslim guerrillas who threatened the small Christian minority to which they belonged. Instead of receiving asylum, however, the Komos were stopped by the US Immigration and Customs Enforcement (ICE) Division of the Department of Homeland Security when they entered North America and were placed in the Hutto detention center. The family was released after a short stay and given asylum.

According to the Global Detention Project (GDP), a nonprofit organization based in Geneva, Switzerland, an estimated 323,591 immigrants were detained in the United States in 2017. Among these, 44,270 were asylum seekers and 59,170 were unaccompanied minors. People of Mexican nationality were the most likely to be detained. There were 6,916 criminal facilities for detaining immigrants in 2018.

Some immigrants are held in jails, some in state prisons, and still others in privately run correctional centers. While the average length of stay for any prisoner is about thirty-seven days, some have remained in detention for several years. If they cannot afford lawyers to help them with their cases, the immigrants receive no legal counsel—unlike American citizens who have a right to legal representation under the US Constitution.

Living conditions at immigrant detention facilities can be dreadful. Women and children live together, while fathers generally must live separately. The Yourdkhanis, refugees from Iran, were another family that was arrested and placed in Hutto.

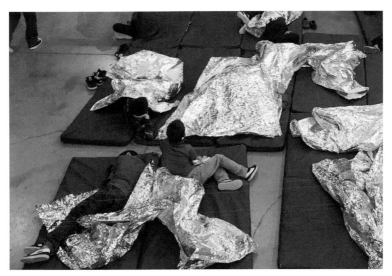

Immigrant children who have been detained by US Customs and Border Protection rest inside a cage in a McAllen, Texas, facility.

Majid Yourdkhani was forced to stay in a separate cell from his wife and daughter; when he became ill, his wife could not help him. Children at Hutto were forced to wear striped suits and were given neither toys nor something as simple as paper and crayons to pass the time. Families were forced to awake at 5:30 a.m., and throughout the night, lights were shone into their cells, making it difficult for anyone to sleep. Children were also disciplined by the staff for running around and yelling—that is, for behaving like children.

In 2007, the American Civil Liberties Union (ACLU), an organization that defends civil rights, sued the Department of Homeland Security over conditions at Hutto. An investigation conducted as part of the lawsuit found that children were forced to live in an environment that was "capable of contributing to the development of unnecessary anxiety and stress [for them]." As a result of the suit, Homeland Security agreed to improve conditions at Hutto. Children were given pajamas to sleep in and toys to play with, and school instruction was increased to seven hours a day from only an hour. In 2009, Hutto became a facility for adult women only.

However, unpleasant conditions remain in other detention facilities. In an interview with the *Cincinnati Enquirer*, a sixteen-year-old Guatemalan immigrant named Edmilson Aguilar Punay recalls his time in a detention center in Phoenix, Arizona. He was housed in a very hot, windowless room with about thirty other boys and men, who had between them access to only one toilet, which wasn't walled off. "Where there were small children, you could hear them crying all the time," said Punay.

One woman held in a detention center in 2018 said she and the other women weren't able to bathe or brush their teeth for eight days. Meanwhile, the women slept beneath "aluminum paper" blankets on the floor. "They treated us so horribly, as though we were animals," she wrote in a letter published on the website of nonprofit Grassroots Leadership. In fact, these centers were commonly called *la perrera* ("the dog pound") by migrants because of the chain-link fences that detained them.

In 2018, the ACLU sued the Trump administration over its family-separation policy, and on June 26, a federal judge ordered that all children younger than five be reunited with their families.

Access to Medical Care

In January 2010, the *New York Times* reported that, since 2003, 107 immigrants had died while in detention. The article noted that, as stated in an investigation conducted by a federal agency, "unbearable, untreated pain had been a significant factor in the suicide" of one detainee, Nery Romero from El Salvador. The investigation found that the staff of the detention center had covered up this problem by making a "fake entry" that said Romero had been given a painkiller. Romero died in a jail in

Bergen County, New Jersey, although a spokesman for that facility would not say whether any changes had been made since the death. At another center, Boubacar Bah, a tailor from Guinea in Africa, suffered a fractured skull, the cause of which was not reported. For thirteen hours, no one called for an ambulance. Bah eventually was taken to a hospital where emergency surgery was performed, but he died anyway.

A 2009 report by Human Rights Watch (HRW) concluded that the medical care in immigrant detention centers was dangerously inadequate, and stated, "Women in detention described violations such as shackling pregnant detainees or failing to follow up on signs of breast and cervical cancer, as well as basic affronts to their dignity." Effective medical treatment was often delayed, and some women were prevented from receiving it due to issues such as inadequate communication and denial of services. Regular exams for cancer and medical care for pregnant women were difficult to obtain for some of the same reasons.

A report by HRW, the ACLU, the National Immigrant Justice Center, and Detention Watch Network studied the deaths of fifteen detainees in ICE custody between December 2015 and April 2017. It found that in eight of these cases, inadequate medical care either caused or contributed to the deaths. In all but one of the cases, in fact, the independent medical experts who conducted the review found "evidence of substandard medical practices."

The *Nation* reports that twelve detainees died while in the custody of the Department of Homeland Security in fiscal year 2017—more than any other year since 2009, and two times the death rate of four years before. One death involved a man who hanged himself within solitary confinement; he had been arrested while exhibiting symptoms of schizophrenia.

The year 2018 saw several reported deaths, including that of a man who committed suicide after being separated from his son.

Detained at Guantánamo Bay

A prisoner at Guantánamo Bay detention camp is led back to his cell after receiving dental treatment.

The United States' presence at Guantánamo Bay dates back to the late 1800s, when US marines were killed there during the Spanish-American War. A few years later, the United States took possession of the 45-square-mile (117-square-km) site on the southeastern end of Cuba and used it as a naval base. Over the years, Guantánamo has been involved in various controversies, though all of them have been overshadowed by the controversies that began in January 2002.

Shortly after the September 11, 2001, terrorist attacks on the United States, President George W. Bush decided to establish a camp at Guantánamo to detain suspected terrorists captured during the president's "war on terror" in Afghanistan, and later Iraq. The first such prisoners arrived at Guantánamo on January 11, 2002. A week later, the government determined that the detainees were terrorists, and therefore they were not entitled to the same liberties as other American prisoners—or even prisoners of war.

Claims that the prisoners were treated inhumanely followed, bolstered by a photo showing the detainees handcuffed, shackled, and on their knees, with their ears, eyes, and mouths covered. Human rights organizations, and eventually the general public, spoke out against the perceived cruel treatment of the detainees. Allegations surfaced that the prisoners were subjected to sexual humiliation, sleep deprivation, a form of mock drowning called waterboarding, and other inhumane acts. Nine detainees died at Guantánamo.

Cries began to surface to shut down the camp, and some prisoners were released. In 2008, the US Supreme Court ruled that the remaining detainees at Guantánamo had the right to challenge their detention in federal court. In January 2009, President Barack Obama ordered the detention center at Guantánamo Bay to be closed within a year. At that time, there were 240 detainees in the facility.

However, the Obama administration never succeeded in closing Guantánamo, as it faced challenges over what to do with those who were considered too dangerous to set free but hard to bring to trial. By 2018, forty detainees were still in Guantánamo, according to the *New York Times*.

Another man, Ronal Francisco Romero, just thirty-nine years old, died of bacterial meningitis while in detention. According to the autopsy, he "would have been intensely, visibly ill and in severe pain for several days" before he was hospitalized.

Waiting for Their Cases to Be Heard

Thousands of those being detained are undocumented immigrants who crossed the southwestern border of the United States. Those who have been caught by immigration officials are being detained until they can be brought into court. These first-time offenders have been told that they will be sent back across the border. However, those caught returning are often given stiffer sentences. As part of Operation Streamline, they can be incarcerated for up to six months.

Federal agents have picked up other undocumented immigrants in raids on employers of illegal immigrants. In 2008, ICE agents raided Agriprocessors, a meatpacking plant in Iowa, and arrested three hundred employees, charging them with being undocumented immigrants. Most were found guilty and sentenced to prisons in Florida and Louisiana.

At one of these facilities in Florida, 2,100 Haitians seeking asylum in the United States were held in detention. In 2006, the detainees reported that they were subject to "overcrowding, filth, beatings, [and] predatory phone prices" to use a pay phone to call family members. In addition, "[s]ome of the prisoners, who [had] already signed their deportation documents, [were] still being held by ICE … Some prisoners [were there] for years awaiting deportation. One [had] been [there] for over three years." As Mark Dow wrote in *Social Research Quarterly*, the immigration detention system is designed to punish those held behind bars.

Some politicians do not have a problem with the mistreatment of undocumented criminals. Former US representative Brian Bilbray, a Republican from California, said, "If they really hate the detention facility, they can always say 'Forget it, I want to go home' [to their own country]. But they see this as a great opportunity to leverage the system so they can stay here legally."

In 2010, the American Bar Association (ABA), America's leading professional association of lawyers, pointed out that judges who hear immigration cases are overwhelmed by the sheer number of them. As a result, those awaiting hearings often spend long periods in detention centers, at a substantial cost to taxpayers. The ABA called for a new court system devoted only to dealing with immigration cases, to speed up the trial process and cut down on detention.

American Jails argued that staff members in jails that house undocumented immigrants, many of whom do not speak English, need to be trained in speaking a foreign language—especially Spanish—so they can respond to emergencies.

The issue of Americans having to learn foreign languages to function in the United States rankles many people. Republican Tim James, who for a time was a candidate for Alabama governor, is one such person. Speaking about his state's practice of printing driver's license exams in twelve different languages, he said, "This is Alabama. We speak English. If you want to live here, learn it. We're only giving that test in English if I'm governor … We welcome non-English speaking people, who are legally in the US, to Alabama. However, if you want to drive in our states, public safety concerns dictate that you need to speak English."

Chapter Seven

LIFE IN PRISON OR PAROLE?

Those who are found guilty of some of the most heinous crimes are often sentenced to life in prison—or, in states where the death penalty is legal, sentenced to death. This means that they don't have the option for parole.

Serial killer Gary Ridgway, also known as the Green River Killer, is currently serving a life sentence without parole for the murders of forty-eight women in Washington State. Prosecutors agreed not to seek the death penalty when Ridgway offered to tell them where all the bodies of his victims were buried. However, they did believe that life without parole was necessary for Ridgway in order to safeguard society and prevent him from jeopardizing the lives of anyone else.

Opposite: Gary Ridgway, commonly known as the Green River Killer, cries as he receives forty-eight life sentences without the chance for parole on December 18, 2003.

What Is a Life Sentence?

Ridgway is one of an estimated 162,000 prisoners serving life sentences in the United States—a number that has almost quintupled since 1984. Ridgway is white, but nearly half of people sentenced to life are African American, constituting one in five of all African American prisoners, according to a 2017 report from the Sentencing Project. Generally, these life sentences are for murder, but they also may be for other crimes, such as rape or drug trafficking.

A life sentence does not always mean exactly what logic would indicate. In states such as Utah or California, a prisoner serving life may be considered for parole in less than ten years. In a state such as Colorado, parole will not be considered for forty to fifty years. However, in several states, including Illinois and Pennsylvania, all life sentences mean just that—there is no possibility of parole.

In those states that allow it, a prisoner can be granted parole only under certain circumstances. Generally, the prisoner's case is reviewed by a parole board, which listens to testimony about his or her behavior behind bars and determines whether he or she is a threat to society. The way parole boards are selected has been criticized. As reported by the Sentencing Project, "[P]arole boards remain the domain of political appointees and two-thirds of states lack any standardized qualifications for service. This has resulted in a highly politicized process that too often discounts evidence and expert testimony." Some states, as a result, have eliminated parole boards. In those states, prisoners must simply serve out their sentence, with no hope of early release.

William Heirens, known as the Lipstick Killer because he wrote a message in lipstick on a wall at the scene of one of his murders, was sentenced to life in Illinois following his conviction for three murders in 1946. In time, he became the first person in Illinois to receive a four-year college degree while in prison. Before he died in 2012, the elderly Heirens had diabetes and spent most of his time in a wheelchair. Though many might have felt that Heirens posed little threat to society, his parole board stated in 2008 that he could not be released. "God will forgive you," a board member said, "but the state won't."

Betty Finn does not sympathize with Heirens either; he killed her six-year-old sister in 1946. "Can you imagine as a child to have this happen?" Finn said. "Can you imagine going to bed at night and all of a sudden your sister is not in her bed? ... He was the bogeyman. I don't think you need to feel sorry for him. He chose his life and he chose his actions ... Keep him locked in jail."

Studies of people over the age of fifty who were released from prison after serving twenty-five years or more showed that relatively few of them ever committed another crime. In fact, the recidivism rate of such people in Ohio was zero, and in Pennsylvania it was only about 1.5 percent. This compares to an overall five-year recidivism rate of roughly 76 percent. "Many lifers are kept in prison long after they represent a public safety threat," said Marc Mauer, executive director of the Sentencing Project.

On the other hand, some of those prisoners who are released do commit more crimes. Reginald McFadden was released from prison in Pennsylvania in 1994 after serving twenty-four years of a life sentence for murder. Soon afterward, he killed at least two more people and was returned to prison to serve a second life sentence. Regardless of how rare it may be, the impact a Reginald McFadden–type case has on the general public—and ultimately on the policies that govern parole cases and the politicians responsible for those policies—can be widespread.

In California, the release of prisoners serving life sentences must be approved by a parole board and then by the governor. Many Americans believe that state officials should be tough on criminals, especially those who have committed violent crimes,

Jasmine Marquez (*right*) talks with Leslie Hoerner (*left*), her probation officer, at the Idaho Department of Correction in 2018.

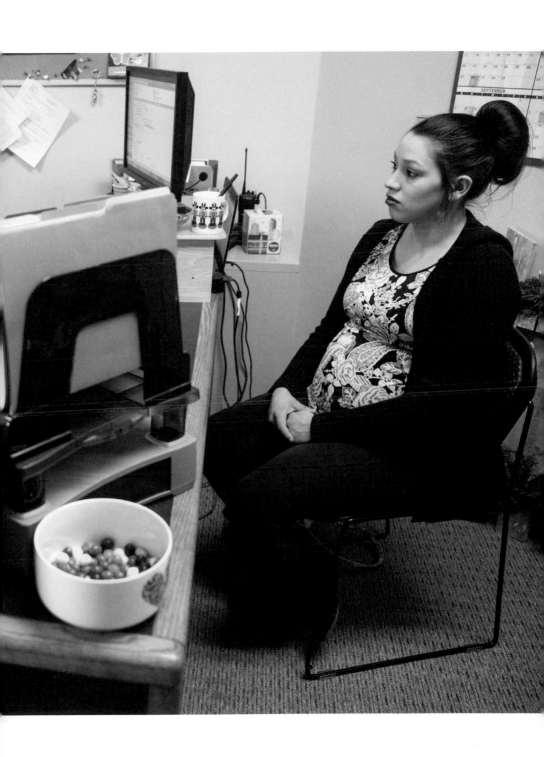

and should not permit them to return to society. However, others argue that if a prisoner has been rehabilitated—like some of those serving life sentences—he or she should be released.

No Chance for Parole

Among those serving life sentences in the United States, about 53,290 had been given no opportunity for parole in 2016, comprising one in twenty-eight prisoners. The largest number of prisoners serving life without parole is incarcerated in Florida. Life without parole is generally reserved for prisoners who have committed murder, such as Gary Ridgway.

In most states, prisoners may serve either a life sentence or life without parole. The two terms can be confusing. "Life without parole" means exactly what it says: those who are given such sentences will spend the rest of their lives behind bars. However, "life sentences" often include indeterminate time frames, such as sentences of "twenty-five years to life." Other life sentences are also open to potential parole. The federal government has eliminated life sentences and only hands down life without parole for particularly violent crimes.

The number of these sentences has increased in response to political pressure placed on politicians for harsher sentencing. In addition, many people oppose the death penalty for moral, religious, financial, and other reasons. Due to the lengthy judicial process necessary to carry out the death penalty, killing a prisoner actually costs more than sentencing him or her to life in prison. People who oppose the death penalty often support a sentence of life without parole as an alternative. In those scenarios, the prisoner remains behind bars and society is protected.

In addition, such a sentence eliminates the chance that a prisoner who has been wrongfully accused of murder may be executed. The possibility of this injustice is another reason many people do not believe in the death penalty.

The Parole System

As of 2018, nearly 2.3 million people were incarcerated in the United States. Millions more are on probation or parole. Probation means that the person lives in the community but is being supervised by a probation officer; many such people have also served time in jail. About 3.7 million individuals are on probation, and about 840,000 people are on parole. Some experts argue that if probation had more services and could be strengthened, more offenders could be in the community than in prison or jail. The Pew Center on the States, a nonprofit research group, estimated that "for hundreds of thousands of lower-level inmates [drug users, for example], incarceration costs taxpayers far more than it saves in prevented crime."

The parole system was designed to help former inmates rehabilitate themselves. As an inmate prepares to be paroled, he or she may become part of a work-release program. This involves working at a job in the community during the day and returning to a correctional facility at night. Other prisoners are released to a halfway house and work at a job but return to close supervision at the halfway house at night. Eventually, they are released to live on their own.

When prisoners are released from prison on parole, they become part of the caseload of a parole officer. The parole officer's responsibility is to monitor the parolee to ensure that he or she abides by the law. This means that the parolee does not commit another crime or violate the conditions of his or her parole by, for instance, failing to show up for periodic meetings with a parole officer. Many prisoners are habitual drug users, and one condition of parole is staying drug- and alcohol-free. To monitor parolees, parole officers administer periodic drug tests. A parolee who fails a test may be returned to prison.

In addition, parole officers are expected to guide parolees into drug rehabilitation programs to help them deal with potential drug problems, aid them in finding counseling for psychological problems, and direct them toward vocational training so they can find jobs. The intent is to keep the parolees from returning to prison, enable them to reform, and keep them in the community.

Unfortunately, these goals frequently aren't met. One reason is that the caseload for each parole officer has greatly increased. More money is being spent on building new prisons than on training and paying for more parole officers, which is an issue of contention for parole officers. One analysis in the *Journal of Offender Rehabilitation* reported that too few officers means that each officer has little time to focus on parolees as individuals and provide counseling or referrals to community agencies. Instead, officers "have little choice but to concentrate on surveillance," wrote Joel Caplan, a PhD candidate at the University of

San Diego judge David Szumowski hears the case of a former nurse who forged a painkiller prescription. She will later be sent to drug court.

Pennsylvania School of Social Policy and Practice. If a parolee violates parole, instead of finding him or her a counselor, a parole officer is more likely to send the person back to prison, simply because it is easier.

A three-month survey conducted in 2017 by the Marshall Project, a nonpartisan news organization focusing on criminal justice, found that 61,250 people in forty-two states were in prison because they broke a rule of their parole, rather than because they committed a new crime.

In testimony before the US Congress in 2009, Stephen Manley, a superior court judge in California, explained that part of the problem was that parole officers are often unable to persuade parolees to comply with the conditions of their release. Most of these released prisoners are not strongly motivated to seek counseling or drug and alcohol rehabilitation. What's more, in many cases, other services—such as mental health counseling— are hard to find. "In my experience," Manley said, "most probation and parole officers direct offenders to find a place to live, get a job, report regularly, enter treatment, drug test, and stay out of trouble. The obligation is put nearly 100% on the offender and if he or she fails to follow directions, the answer is often more punishment."

These offenders often cannot easily access treatment and therefore continue to use drugs, which is a violation of their parole or probation. What's more, one study by Dr. Faye Taxman at George Mason University found most treatment options available are not very good and therefore people do not get much help anyway. The study found that the probation and parole system was not preventing reincarceration and that expanding treatment services in the community would help tremendously.

To deal with this problem, many states have begun relying on drug courts. The concept originated in Florida in 1989 and had grown to more than 3,100 programs nationwide as of May 2018. The drug court idea has shown that treatment can be more

An Alternative Program for Parolees

Many parolees come out of prison with few, if any, resources. They may have no place to live and suffer from psychological illnesses as well as drug and alcohol addictions. With large caseloads, parole officers are often unable to monitor technical parole violations if parolees do not show up for drug treatment programs and continue using drugs. In addition, technical violations usually involve costly and time-consuming hearings. Parole officers with heavy caseloads may not have time to address these violations unless they get help.

To deal with this problem, the federal government has established the Court Services and Offender Supervision Agency (CSOSA) for Washington, DC. Parolees know that if they commit a violation, various punishments will be used. Parolees may be monitored with electronic ankle bracelets, or they may be placed in the Re-Entry and Sanctions Center. This center, which has room for more than one hundred residents, provides a twenty-eight-day program of counseling. It is aimed at inmates who have just been released from prison and have a high risk of returning for additional offenses. After this program, most parolees are immediately referred to a drug-treatment facility for continued counseling.

CSOSA has also instituted a 180-day treatment program in a facility for offenders who have returned to drug abuse or who have been guilty of another technical violation of their parole. What's more, its vocational program helps parolees train for jobs in areas such as food services and construction. This is another way of helping parolees avoid being sent back to prison.

CSOSA has a profound effect on residents of the District of Columbia, one in seventy of whom are supervised by the agency on any given day. Of those within its care, 63 percent complete the program successfully.

effective than just prison or jail. In this type of program, the court works with a parole officer and community rehabilitation services to monitor the parolee and provide counseling and treatment. The parolee is subject to regular drug testing, and if found in violation of parole, is immediately brought in front of a judge. The judge warns the parolee that continued violations can result in a return to prison. Studies in California and New York have shown that drug courts have significantly cut recidivism rates.

Drug courts, according to the National Association of Drug Court Professionals (NADCP), serve 150,000 people every year. "By being immersed in the drug court continuum of care, my desire to stay sober became greater than my desire to use," one drug-court graduate told the NADCP, which testifies that more than a million people total have been treated in such courts, with $13,000 in criminal-justice and crime-related costs saved per participant.

Parolees not only need help in the community, they also require programs while in prison to prepare them for release. Almost all federal facilities offer vocational training, but only 44 percent of private prisons and 7 percent of jails offer them. Training in preparation for post-release work, however, can be critical, since research has shown that a parolee who has a job and is earning an income is less likely to be rearrested for committing a crime, such as selling drugs to make money.

Rehabilitation programs both inside and outside of prisons, advocates hope, can transform communities, keep people safer, and lower costs within the criminal justice system—all at the same time. Still, the debate continues over whether—or if—such programs should continue or expand.

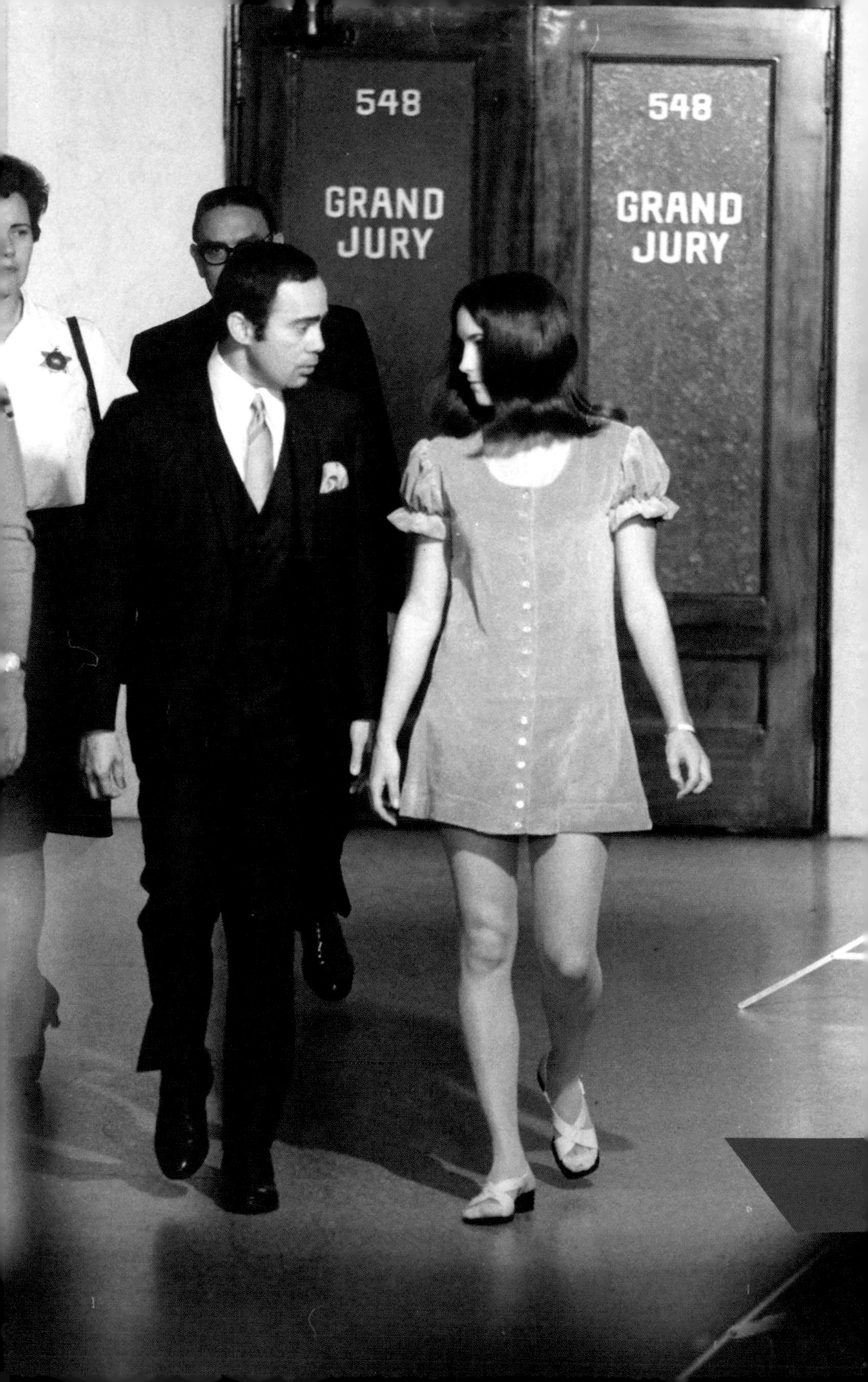

Chapter Eight

CHOOSING BETWEEN REHABILITATION AND PUNISHMENT

The question of whether prisons serve to punish or rehabilitate inmates yields few black-and-white answers. Many or even most people would likely agree they should do both. The debate, then, centers around whether prisons have become too comfortable for inmates in their attempt to offer rehabilitation and around what types of rehabilitation are most effective at reducing costs and preventing future crime.

Some, however, insist that no rehabilitation should take place at all and that those who have committed horrendous crimes are locked up to protect the rest of society, not to be reformed. In the case of such brutal criminals as Susan Atkins, it can be easy to understand this

Opposite: Murderer Susan Atkins (*right*) speaks with her attorney, Richard Caballero (*second from right*), after testifying before a grand jury in December 1969. Atkins was later sentenced to life in prison.

perspective. Still, the question of what role mercy plays in the criminal justice system remains a matter of debate.

Mercy and Justice

Susan Atkins confessed to her most notorious crime. In 1969, she said, she held down pregnant actress Sharon Tate and stabbed her sixteen times in Tate's home in Los Angeles. Before leaving the crime scene, Atkins used Tate's blood to write the word "PIG" on the front door. In 1993, Atkins described Tate's last words. "She asked me to let the baby live," Atkins said. "I told her I didn't have mercy for her." At her trial years earlier, Atkins said, "[I have] no guilt for what I've done. It was right then and I still believe it was right."

Atkins, who committed the crime as part of Charles Manson's "family" of followers, was convicted of the murder of Tate and seven others. She was sent to prison to serve a life sentence. Over the years, Atkins received thirteen parole hearings and was denied her freedom at each of them, despite claims that she was remorseful and had become a Christian, as well as reports from staff that she had been a near-perfect prisoner.

Because of the brutality of her crimes, no one ever believed Atkins had a chance to get out of prison. But, prior to her thirteenth attempt at parole in September 2009, some people's opinions had changed. There were those who believed Atkins should be released and actually might have a chance to be because she was terminally ill with brain cancer and unlikely to live much longer. Her family argued that she should be allowed to die at home and that the state would save $10,000 a day in medical costs if they released her. Her husband, whom she had married while she was in prison, said, "She's paralyzed [over] just about 85 percent of her body. She can nod her head and she can look left and right and she has limited use of her left arm." Even Vincent Bugliosi, the prosecutor who had helped convict Atkins four decades earlier, believed she should be released. He said, "She's already paid substantially for her crime, close to 40 years behind bars. She has terminal cancer. The mercy she [is] asking for is so minuscule. She's about to die. It's not like we're going to see her down at Disneyland."

Even after watching Atkins wheeled into the parole hearing in a hospital bed, Tate's family did not budge from the stance they had held the previous four decades—that Atkins should die in prison for what she did. Sharon Tate's younger sister, Debra Tate, told the parole board she "will pray for [Atkins's] soul when she draws her last breath, but until then I think she should remain in this controlled situation." Steve Chapman, a noted syndicated columnist for the *Chicago Tribune*, chimed in on the case:

> [M]aybe there is money to be saved by letting ... Atkins out of their taxpayer-financed housing. But few government funds were ever better spent. And it's hard to see why people who have committed violent crimes deserve any consideration beyond the fair trial and sentencing they have already gotten. Compassionate release is compassionate only to criminals, not their victims.

In Atkins's case, the compassion approach did not work, possibly due in part to the high-profile status and horrific nature of her crimes. She was again denied parole and died less than a month later.

However, there are instances in which prisoners in the United States have been released under special circumstances. In fact, the Federal Bureau of Prisons has a policy relating to that very issue. It is called compassionate release, and it allows an inmate the right to appeal to his or her warden for release during "particularly extraordinary or compelling circumstances which could not reasonably have been foreseen by the court at the time of sentencing." Such a request must be fairly specific, and several officials must approve it before the release can be granted.

Suffering from cancer, Cinderella Marrett was granted such a release in New York in 2009. Just two years earlier, Marrett, then in her early seventies, had been caught smuggling cocaine in her girdle at a New York airport. During Marrett's parole hearing, her daughter argued that Marrett only had the cocaine to help offset the cost of her medical expenses. Once granted parole, Marrett was released to a nursing home. She died early the next year.

The Rights of Victims

There are groups designed specifically to speak for victims when they cannot speak for themselves, or even when they can. Over the years, victims' rights have become central to the debate over prison reform, and the federal government has enacted several laws that guarantee rights to victims of crime. In 1975, a nonprofit group, the National Organization for Victim Assistance, was founded to promote the rights of crime victims throughout the United States. Today, every state has a similar type of group. These groups often advocate for the victims of crime in many settings, including in the legislature, in the courtroom, and at parole hearings. Many groups even provide financial support for victims.

Miriam Shehane is one such victims' advocate. She became involved in victims' rights, as many other people have done, after suffering a personal tragedy. In 1976, Shehane's twenty-one-year-old daughter was abducted from a convenience store parking lot in Alabama, then raped and murdered. Shehane subsequently began the victims' rights movement in Alabama by forming Victims of

Sandra Hudson (*right*) and Alabama attorney general Troy King embrace at a candlelight vigil held by Victims of Crime and Leniency.

Crime and Leniency in 1982 as a way of helping her deal with the pain of her loss. In her view, criminals give up their rights to any compassion the moment they are convicted of their crimes. "I would like to know that the two serving time in prison for killing my daughter have to think they're not in a place that is a place to reside with the comforts of home," she told author Sasha Abramsky in 2005. "Are they able to touch [visitors]? I would hope not. I would like to know they had to pay for their housing. They should have to grow their own food." Shehane went on to say that she believed more people, killers and rapists included, should be executed for their crimes, and that "[i]t should be a shameful thing to be incarcerated—and it's not anymore."

Ted Deeds of the Law Enforcement Alliance of America, a strong advocate for the rights of victims, agreed that prison should not be easy and the goal is to punish criminals. He said, "Prisons have become mini-resorts and it's disgusting, and it's particularly disgusting to crime victims. We strongly believe that prison is meant to be punishment, a deterrent and a prevention tool, not a resort experience."

The Argument for Compassion

Finances play a large role in the debate over who should be locked up and for how long. It is expensive to keep prisoners behind bars, especially those who require special medical attention. Releasing some of them from prison, compassion advocates say, would change who pays for the medical treatment. In Shehane's home state of Alabama, for example, it costs roughly $65,000 per year to treat terminally ill or infirm inmates on average. That money comes from the prison system. Allowing such inmates to be released would shift the cost of their care to the federally funded Medicare program or the state- and federally funded Medicaid program. Victims' rights advocates respond that, in the end, taxpayers still pay for the cost, so no money is really saved by releasing terminally ill inmates and they should stay behind bars.

The issue of whether or not inmates deserve compassion is not topical only when the prisoner is critically ill and has petitioned for a compassionate release. There are people who believe prison is a punishment and that those serving time do not deserve much consideration at all. After all, they argue, no compassion was shown for the victims, so why should there be any shown to the perpetrators? Offering prisoners opportunities for educational, counseling, and job training does not amount to punishment—it amounts to compassion, and criminals do not deserve any, they say.

Politics also play a large role in what happens inside prison walls. Many politicians will not openly advocate for punishing criminals because being perceived as not caring for fellow human beings would be damaging to their careers. Instead, politicians indirectly increase the punishment prisoners receive while behind bars by voting to slash prison budgets. This has happened many times over the past few years, due to the country's extended economic downturn. Republican victories during the midterm elections of 2010 and in the presidential election of 2016 helped swing the country toward a more tough-on-crime stance. After 2010, newly elected officials in several states proposed major cuts to prison budgets. In Florida, Governor Rick Scott proposed cutting the state's $2.5 billion prison budget by $1 billion a year. Proponents of the proposal found benefits in the savings. Opponents pictured their streets full of recently released criminals.

Exactly where the general public stands on compassion versus punishment for prisoners is not easy to determine. In 2012, the most recent year for which such data was available, a survey conducted by Public Opinion Strategies and the Mellman Group found that 69 percent of Americans agreed that "[t]here are more effective, less expensive alternatives to prison for non-violent offenders and expanding those alternatives is the best way to reduce the crime rate." In comparison, 25 percent believed that "[p]eople who commit crimes belong behind bars, end of story." On average, voters believed that about 20 percent of prisoners could be released without compromising public safety.

Dealing with Overcrowding

Releasing prisoners early isn't just done for reasons of compassion. In 2011, overcrowding problems in California prisons had reached a state of crisis, with some prisons reaching nearly 300 percent of their maximum capacity. So that year, the state took a seemingly drastic step, and over a period of fifteen months, released more than 27,500 inmates from prison, either putting them on parole or sending them to county jails.

Some worried that such mass releases of prisoners could endanger the public, leading to increases in crime. However, two studies released in 2016 found that the release of these prisoners had not created any significant change in the crime rate. In fact, one study concluded that "[a]n astounding 17 percent reduction in the size of the California prison population ... had no effect on aggregate rates of violent or property crime."

Since the overcrowding problem reached a head, Californians also passed Proposition 47, which changed some felony-level drug crimes to misdemeanors, effectively reducing sentences for them. Releasing certain types of offenders, it seemed, had addressed the overcrowding issue in a way that did not endanger the public or make them feel significantly less safe.

Interestingly, a study published in 2006 in the journal *Criminology & Public Policy* investigated whether the increase in incarceration actually improves public safety—that is, reduces crime. Looking at prison and crime statistics from 1972 through 2000, the study found that the effect of prison growth on crime diminishes as the scale of imprisonment increases. The scale tips away from reducing crime once the rate of imprisonment reaches about 325 prisoners per 100,000. Beyond that, increasing the rate of incarceration does not impact crime figures. One of the reasons for this is that new inmates admitted in the past when prison populations were small tended to be primarily violent and property offenders. Removing such people from society obviously would have an impact on crime in communities. But recently, prisoners have tended to be mainly drug offenders. Removing them from society has had a smaller effect on crime rates in communities, the study showed.

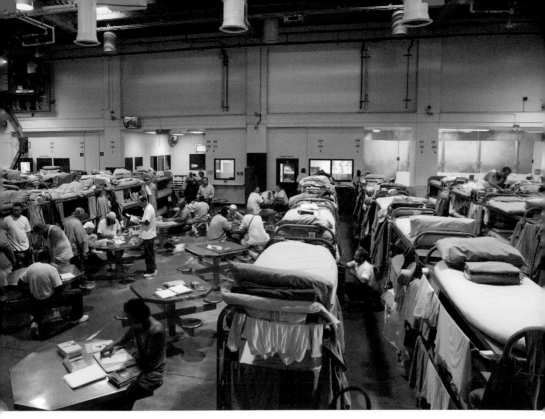

Mule Creek State Prison inmates are living in a gymnasium in 2007 as California prison overcrowding reaches a head.

Reducing Costs Through Privatization

The Great Recession of 2007–2009 led states to look for alternative ways to deal with poor prison conditions and the shortage of funds available to improve them. Many offered up the solution of letting private companies, rather than state or federal governments, operate prisons.

However, some legislators are skeptical about the impact of privatizing prisons. In the past, when efforts at privatization were made, states did not realize large savings. In addition, some prison officials are worried that private facilities cannot properly deal with violent criminals. James Austin, who helped lead a study

Speaking to Prisoners

In her book, *Dreams from the Monster Factory: A Tale of Prison, Redemption, and One Woman's Fight to Restore Justice to All,* Sunny Schwartz wrote about an innovative prison program that she founded in California in 1997. Her program, Resolve to Stop the Violence Project (RSVP), has reduced recidivism significantly during the two decades that it has operated. In fact, according to the RSVP website, "After 16 weeks in RSVP there are 82% lower rearrests for violent crimes during the first year after release compared to the general population within the San Francisco county jail system."

The program aims to serve men held in San Francisco Jail who are willing to stop being violent against those around them. In group therapy sessions, prisoners are urged to confront the ways in which they have hurt other people—family, friends, and victims. The program helps prisoners recognize what they have done, take responsibility for their actions, and even admit to family and friends the harm that they may have caused them.

Don, a bank robber, recognized that he had a drug problem but refused to confront his own violent behavior. The RSVP program helped him acknowledge and deal with his anger and violence. He is just one of the prisoners whom RSVP has helped.

by the Department of Justice, explained that private companies have experience with minimum- and medium-security prisons but not with maximum-security facilities.

More than two dozen states work with private prison companies such as Management and Training Corporation, the company that operates the East Mississippi Correctional Facility mentioned at the beginning of chapter 4. The number of people housed in such facilities has increased by 45 percent since 2000, although the number of prisoners during that time rose only 10 percent. States such as Mississippi require that private facilities function at 10 percent lower cost than prisons run by the state. That saves money, but some allege it also leads to dangerous levels of understaffing, the *New York Times* reports.

In 2016, a report by the Justice Department found that privately operated prisons are more violent for both inmates and guards than government-run institutions. The Barack Obama administration aimed to phase out privatization on a federal level, but Jeff Sessions, then attorney general for President Donald Trump, reversed those efforts. The Trump administration has called for expanding their use.

Justice for All

As 2018 came to a close, a new bill was making its way through Congress. The First Step Act aimed to incentivize inmates to participate in more rehabilitation and vocational programs, and it would provide more funding for such programs. It would increase the number of credits for good conduct an inmate could earn. It would decrease the power of mandatory minimums and potentially reduce the sentences of people convicted of crack cocaine–related offenses before 2010. (Such prosecutions unfairly jailed a higher percentage of African Americans.) It would take some compassionate measures, such as ensuring that prisoners

Incarceration: Punishment or Rehabilitation?

An estimated four hundred prisoners caused a disturbance and took two guards hostage on July 9, 2017, at the Great Plains Correctional Facility in Oklahoma, pictured here.

are housed closer to their families—a rule already in effect but often not enforced. President Trump announced his support for the bill.

Critics of the bill said it didn't go far enough, insisting that sentencing laws needed further reforming to avoid excessive sentences. Only then, critics said, could the country's high incarceration rate be significantly reduced. They also pointed out that many provisions would only affect federal prisoners, a relatively small percentage of the overall imprisoned population in the United States.

No matter what happens with the bill, says Kara Gotsch, director of strategic initiatives at the Sentencing Project, there will still be "so much more to do." Building a prison system that is both effective and just for all involved requires constant improvements, especially as new challenges arise. For now, it seems, the debate will continue.

Glossary

adjudicate To make a decision about; to act as judge.

asylum Protection afforded to refugees by another nation or agency.

controversy An ongoing public dispute or debate.

correctional Of or related to the system designed to punish, reform, or rehabilitate those who have committed a crime.

delinquent A young person who performs illegal acts.

embezzle To steal something for one's own use.

guerrilla A person who engages in irregular warfare, especially as part of an independent unit conducting sabotage.

immigrant A person who migrates to a different country from where he or she was born, usually to live there permanently.

incarceration Confinement in a jail or prison.

juvenile A child or teenager who is not legally an adult.

larceny The unlawful taking of personal property.

offense Crime.

parole A conditional release of a prisoner.

preponderance Excess number or quantity.

probation The act of suspending a criminal's sentence in exchange for good behavior.

psychiatry The study of the human mind.

recidivism Relapse into criminal behavior; return to prison because of such behavior.

rehabilitation Restoration of someone to a useful place in society.

restitution Giving the equivalent of some injury to a victim.

truancy Nonattendance of school.

vocational training Classes to learn the skills for a particular profession.

Further Information

Books

Bauer, Shane. *American Prison: A Reporter's Undercover Journey into the Business of Punishment*. New York: Penguin Press, 2018.

Jiang Stein, Deborah. *Prison Baby: A Memoir.* New York: Beacon Press: 2014.

Senghor, Shaka. *Writing My Wrongs: Life, Death, and Redemption in an American Prison*. New York: Drop a Gem Publishing, LLC, 2016.

Spanne, Autumn, Nora McCarthy, and Laura Longhine, eds. *Wish You Were Here: Teens Write About Parents in Prison*. New York: Youth Communication, New York Center, 2010.

Websites

The Bureau of Justice Statistics

https://www.bjs.gov

This US governmental resource offers key statistics and information about incarceration, probation, and parole in the United States.

The Marshall Project

https://www.themarshallproject.org

This nonprofit, nonpartisan news organization provides useful research and analysis on the US criminal justice system.

Prison Policy Initiative

https://www.prisonpolicy.org

This nonpartisan, nonprofit organization conducts research on mass criminalization and aims to achieve a more just society. The website offers a wealth of statistics and information on incarceration in the United States.

Videos

Forgotten Youth: Inside America's Prisons

https://www.aljazeera.com/programmes/faultlines/2015/09/forgotten-youth-america-prisons-150915093857683.html

This twenty-five-minute video from Al Jazeera investigates how juveniles are treated in US prisons.

Mass Incarceration in the US

https://www.youtube.com/watch?v=NaPBcUUqbew

This motion graphic features research from the Prison Policy Initiative and offers key data on incarceration in the United States.

Why the U.S. Has More Prisoners Than Any Other Country

https://www.youtube.com/watch?v=orVVttsJmPY

This video offers insight on why the United States' prison population is so high compared to that of the rest of the world.

Organizations

Correctional Service of Canada
National Headquarters
340 Laurier Avenue West
Ottawa, ON K1A 0P9
Canada
(613) 992-5891
https://www.canada.ca/en/correctional-service.html

This agency of the Canadian federal government is tasked with administering prison sentences and managing detention facilities.

National Institute of Justice
810 Seventh Street NW
Washington, DC 20531
(202) 307-0703
https://www.nij.gov
NIJ uses scientific study and analysis to improve criminal and juvenile justice practices and reduce crime.

Office of Juvenile Justice and Delinquency Prevention
810 Seventh Street NW
Washington, DC 20531
(202) 307–5911

http://www.ojjdp.gov

The US Congress has tasked the OJJDP with improving juvenile justice policies and practices, improving public safety, and offering key services to juveniles and families.

PASAN

526 Richmond Street E

Toronto, ON M5A 1R3

Canada

(416) 920-9567

This community-based organization offers support, education, and HIV/HCV–prevention services to prisoners, former prisoners, and their families.

US Department of Justice

950 Pennsylvania Avenue NW

Washington, DC 20530-0001

(202) 353-1555

http://justice.gov

This department of the federal government is responsible for upholding the law and seeking "just punishment for those guilty of unlawful behavior."

US Immigration and Customs Enforcement

500 12th Street SW

Washington, DC 20536

(866) 347-2423

http://www.ice.gov

This US federal agency, called ICE for short, enforces laws around customs, border patrol, trade, and public safety. It has more than twenty thousand employees.

Bibliography

"About the Prison Education Program." Boston University Metropolitan College. Accessed November 17, 2018. http://sites.bu.edu/pep/about.

Abramsky, Sasha. *American Furies: Crime, Punishment, and Vengeance in the Age of Mass Imprisonment.* Boston: Beacon Press, 2007.

Ahlin, Eileen M. "Risk Factors of Sexual Assault and Victimization Among Youth in Custody." *Journal of Interpersonal Violence* (February 16, 2018). https://journals.sagepub.com/eprint/ Sq2m5xEM6ZpRstW4RyFs/full#articleCitationDownloadContainer.

The American Prison. New York: The American Correctional Association, 1983.

Anapol, Avery. "Immigrant Teen Describes Conditions in Phoenix ICE Detention Center." *Hill*, June 22, 2018. https://thehill.com/ latino/393705-immigrant-teen-describes-conditions-in-ice-detention-center.

Armour, Jeff, and Sarah Hammond. "Minority Youth in the Juvenile Justice System: Disproportionate Minority Contact." National Conference of State Legislatures, January 2009. www.ncsl.org/print/cj/minoritiesinjj.pdf.

Associated Press. "Louisiana Boosts Money for Prisoner Rehabilitation Programs." KLFY, October 18, 2018. https://www.klfy.com/news/ louisiana/louisiana-boosts-money-for-prisoner-rehabilitation-programs/1534357983.

Avila, Jim, and Felicia Patinkin. "Susan Atkins on Quest for Parole, Forty Years After Charles Manson Murders." ABC News, August 7, 2009. http://abcnews.go.com/GMA/MansonMurders/ story?id=8240770&page=1.

Badger, Emily, Claire Cain Miller, Adam Pearce, and Kevin Quealy.
"Extensive Data Shows Punishing Reach of Racism for Black Boys."
New York Times, March 19, 2018. https://www.nytimes.com/
interactive/2018/03/19/upshot/race-class-white-and-black-men.html.

Barry, Dan, Miriam Jordan, Annie Correal, and Manny Fernandez.
"Cleaning Toilets, Following Rules: A Migrant Child's Days in
Detention." *New York Times*, July 14, 2018. https://www.nytimes.
com/2018/07/14/us/migrant-children-shelters.html.

Bernstein, Nina. "Officials Obscured Truth of Migrant Deaths in Jail." *New
York Times*, January 10, 2010. https://www.nytimes.com/2010/01/10/
us/10detain.html.

Bigham, Will. "Conviction of Inmate Abuse Reinstated for Calif. Officer."
Inland Valley Daily Bulletin, June 8, 2010. http://www.correctionsone.
com/arrests-and-sentencing/articles/2079934-Conviction-of-inmate-
abuse-reinstated-for-Calif-officer.

Blum, Jeff. "Identifying and Treating Mental Illness: One Jail System's
Story." *Corrections Today* (August 2007). https://www.in.gov/idoc/
unlockingthemystery/articles/jailstory1.pdf.

Caplan, Joel M. "Parole System Anomie: Conflicting Models of Casework
and Surveillance." United States Courts, December 2006. http://
www.uscourts.gov/federal-probation-journal/2006/12/parole-system-
anomie-conflicting-models-casework-and-surveillance.

Carson, E. Ann. "Aging of the State Prison Population, 1993–2013."
Bureau of Justice Statistics, May 19, 2016. https://www.bjs.gov/
index.cfm?ty=pbdetail&iid=5602.

Caygle, Heather, and Elana Schor. "Cotton Jolts Prison Reform
Negotiations." *Politico*, May 18, 2018. https://www.politico.com/
story/2018/05/18/tom-cotton-prison-reform-negotiations-598031.

Chapman, Steve. "Let Us Ask Whether Their Victims Were Shown Compassion." *Gaston Gazette*, September 28, 2009. http://www.gastongazette.com/articles/ask-38427-compassion-let.html.

Chen, Michelle. "More Immigrants Died in Detention in Fiscal Year 2017 Than in Any Year Since 2009." *Nation*, June 20, 2018. https://www.thenation.com/article/immigrants-died-detention-fiscal-year-2017-year-since-2009.

Chen, Stephanie. "Prison Health-Care Costs Rise as Inmates Grow Older and Sicker." CNN, November 13, 2008. http://articles.cnn.com/2009-11-13/justice/aging.inmates_1_prison-inmate-largest-prison-systems-medical-costs?_s=PM:CRIME.

Cheng, Amrit. "Family Separation in Court: What You Need to Know." American Civil Liberties Union, July 10, 2018. https://www.aclu.org/blog/immigrants-rights/immigrants-rights-and-detention/family-separation-court-what-you-need-know.

Cole, David. "Can Our Shameful Prisons Be Reformed?" *New York Review of Books*, November 19, 2009. https://www.nybooks.com/articles/2009/11/19/can-our-shameful-prisons-be-reformed.

"Compassionate Release; Procedures for Implementation of 18 U.S.C 3582 (c) (1) (A) & 4205 (g)." Department of Justice, Federal Bureau of Prisons, May 19, 1998. http://www.bop.gov/policy/progstat/5050_046.pdf.

Condon, Stephanie. "Alabama Gov. Candidate Tim James: 'We Speak English. If You Want to Live Here, Learn It.'" CBS News, http://www.cbsnews.com/8301-503544_162-20003524-503544.html.

Confessore, Nicholas. "Four Youth Prisons in New York Used Excessive Force." *New York Times*, August 25, 2009. https://www.nytimes.com/2009/08/25/nyregion/25juvenile.html.

"Corrections Officers Describe a Difficult, Stressful Job and Conditions That Put Staff and Prisoners at Risk." Commission on Safety and Abuse in America's Prisons, 2005. www.prisoncommission.org/pres_release_110105.asp.

Cox, Stephen. *The Big House.* New Haven, CT: Yale University Press, 2009.

"Criminal Justice Facts." Sentencing Project, 2017. Criminal Justice Facts. https://www.sentencingproject.org/criminal-justice-facts.

"Criminal Justice Fact Sheet." NAACP, 2018. https://www.naacp.org/criminal-justice-fact-sheet.

"CSOSA." Court Services and Offender Supervision Agency. Accessed November 18, 2018. https://www.csosa.gov.

Cuizon, Gwendolyn. "Education in Prison." *Educational Issues* (February 13, 2009). http://educationalissues.suite101.com/article.cfm/education_in_prison.

DiFilippo, Dana. "Growing Old Behind Bars." *Philadelphia Daily News*, May 8, 2006.

Domanick, Joe. "Anatomy of a Prison." *Los Angeles Magazine*, September 4, 2009.

Dow, Mark. "Designed to Punish: Immigrant Detention and Deportation." *Social Research* (Summer 2007).

"Drug Courts." US Department of Justice, Office of Justice Programs, May 2018. https://www.ncjrs.gov/pdffiles1/nij/238527.pdf.

"The Economic Impact of Prison Rehabilitation Programs." University of Pennsylvania Penn Wharton Public Policy Initiative, August 17, 2017. https://publicpolicy.wharton.upenn.edu/live/news/2059-the-economic-impact-of-prison-rehabilitation/for-students/blog/news.php#_edn1.

Epstein, Helen. "America's Prisons: Is There Hope?" *New York Review of Books*, June 11, 2009. https://www.nybooks.com/articles/2009/06/11/americas-prisons-is-there-hope.

Erickson, Bo, and Ed O'Keefe. "Government Had No Organized Plan for Separated Children at Border, Says Watchdog." CBS News, October 24, 2018. https://www.cbsnews.com/news/government-had-no-organized-plan-for-separated-children-at-border-says-watchdog.

Estelle v. Gamble. Cornell University Law School. http://www4.law.cornell.edu/ supct/html/ historics/USSC_CR_0429_0097_ZS.html.

"Facts About Prison and People in Prison." Sentencing Project, August 2017. https://www.sentencingproject.org/wp-content/uploads/2016/02/Facts-About-Prisons.pdf.

Falcon, Gabriel. "'Lipstick Killer' Behind Bars Since 1946." CNN, October 25, 2009. http://www.cnn.com/2009/CRIME/10/24/illinois.lipstick.murders/index.html.

Fantz, Ashley. "Girls Behind Bars Tell Their Stories." CNN, March 26, 2015. https:// www.cnn.com/2015/03/26/us/cnnphotos-girls-behind-bars/index.html.

"Feds Begin Tracking Sexual Violence in Juvenile Jails." Contemporary Sexuality (October 2008).

Feltz, Renee. "A New Migration Policy: Producing Felons for Profit." NACLA Report on the Americas, November/December 2008.

Ferro, Jeffrey. *Prisons*. New York: Facts on File, 2006.

Furness, Jill. "Fighting for the Futures of Young Offenders," *Corrections Today* 3 (June 2009).

Gaes, Gerald. "The Impact of Prison Education Programs on Post-Release Outcomes." Reentry Roundtable on Education, February 18, 2008.

Gass, Nick. "Sen. Tom Cotton: U.S. Has 'Under-Incarceration Problem.'" *Politico*, May 19, 2016. https://www.politico.com/story/2016/05/tom-cotton-under-incarceration-223371.

George, Justin. "What's Really in the First Step Act?" Marshall Project, November 16, 2018. https://www.themarshallproject.org/2018/11/16/what-s-really-in-the-first-step-act.

Gilson, Dave. "What We Know About Violence in America's Prisons." *Mother Jones*, July/August 2016. https://www.motherjones.com/politics/2016/06/attacks-and-assaults-behind-bars-cca-private-prisons.

Gramlich, John. "America's Incarceration Rate Is at a Two-Decade Low." Pew Research Center, May 2, 2018. http://www.pewresearch.org/fact-tank/2018/05/02/americas-incarceration-rate-is-at-a-two-decade-low.

"Green River Killer Avoids Death in Plea Deal." CNN, 2003. http://www.cnn.com/2003/LAW/11/05/green.river.killings.

Gross, Daniel A. "An Inside Account of the National Prisoners' Strike." *New Yorker*, September 6, 2018. https://www.newyorker.com/news/as-told-to/an-inside-account-of-the-national-prisoners-strike.

"The Guantánamo Docket: Held." *New York Times*. Accessed November 18, 2018. https://www.nytimes.com/interactive/projects/guantanamo/detainees/held.

Gumbel, Andrew. "America Has 2,000 Young Offenders Serving Life Terms in Jail." *Independent*, October 12, 2005. https://www.independent.co.uk/news/world/americas/america-has-2000-young-offenders-serving-life-terms-in-jail-318840.html.

Hager, Eli. "At Least 61,000 Nationwide Are in Prison for Minor Parole Violations." Marshall Project, April 23, 2017. https://www.themarshallproject.org/2017/04/23/at-least-61-000-nationwide-are-in-prison-for-minor-parole-violations.

Hartman, Kenneth. "The Recession Behind Bars." *New York Times*, September 6, 2009.

"Higher Education Behind Bars: Postsecondary Prison Education Programs Make a Difference." American Council on Education, October 14, 2008.

Hoffman, Clyde. "California Blasted for Poor Prison Health Care." *All Things Considered*, NPR, October 14, 2004. http://www.npr.org/templates/story/story.php?storyId=4109523.

House Appropriations Subcommittee on Commerce, Justice, and Science, Challenges Facing Federal Prisons. Congressional testimony of Bryan Lowry, March 10, 2009.

House Appropriations Subcommittee on Commerce, Justice, and Science, Innovative Prisoner Re-Entry Programs. Congressional testimony of Stephen Manley, March 11, 2009.

Infantino, Joe. "California Turns a Corner in Effort to Regain Prison Health Care Oversight." California Healthline, October 15, 2015. https://californiahealthline.org/news/california-turns-a-corner-in-effort-to-regain-prison-health-care-oversight.

Inter-American Commission on Human Rights. "The Situation of Children in the Adult Criminal Justice System in the United States." Organization of American States, March 1, 2018. http://www.oas.org/en/iachr/reports/pdfs/Children-USA.pdf.

Jackson, David, Deborah Barfield Berry, and John Fritze. "Trump Embraces Bipartisan Criminal Justice Reform Legislation." *USA TODAY*, November 14, 2018. https://www.usatoday.com/story/news/politics/2018/11/14/donald-trump-embraces-criminal-justice-reform-package-congress/2000991002.

Jackman, Tom. "Mass Reduction of California Prison Population Didn't Cause Rise in Crime, Two Studies Find." *Washington Post*, May 18, 2016. https://www.washingtonpost.com/news/true-crime/wp/2016/05/18/

mass-release-of-california-prisoners-didnt-cause-rise-in-crime-two-studies-find/?utm_term=.b59aadb7e86d.

"Justice for All: National Drug Court Month, May 2018." National Association of Drug Court Professionals, May 2018. https://www.nadcp.org/wp-content/uploads/2018/04/National-Drug-Court-Month-Field-Kit-2018_final.pdf.

"Juvenile Justice." National Alliance on Mental Illness. Accessed November 17, 2018. https://www.nami.org/Learn-More/Mental-Health-Public-Policy/Juvenile-Justice.

"Juvenile Residential Facility Census Databook: 2000–2016." National Center for Juvenile Justice. Accessed November 17, 2018. https://www.ojjdp.gov/ojstatbb/jrfcdb/asp/selection_profile.asp.

Karson, Jill, ed. *Criminal Justice: Opposing Viewpoints*. San Diego, CA: Greenhaven, 1998.

Kaufman, Pat. "Prison Rape: Research Explores Prevalence, Prevention." *NIJ Journal* (March 2008). https://www.nij.gov/journals/259/Pages/prison-rape.aspx.

Kopan, Tal. "New Questions Raised on Trump's Family Separations as 14 Children Discovered." *San Francisco Chronicle*, October 26, 2018. https://www.sfchronicle.com/politics/article/New-questions-raised-on-Trump-s-family-13338722.php.

LaCourse Jr., R. David. "Three Strikes in Review." Washington Policy Center, 1997.

Lee, W. Storrs. "Stone Walls Do Not a Prison Make." *American Heritage*, 2 (February 1967). http://www.americanheritage.com/articles/magazine/ah/1967/2/1967_2_40.shtml.

Liedka, R., A. Piehl, and B. Useem. "The Crime-Control Effect of Incarceration: Does Scale Matter?" *Criminology and Public Policy* (May 2006): 245–276.

Liptak, Adam. "To More Inmates, Life Term Means Dying Behind Bars." *New York Times*, October 2, 2005. https://www.nytimes.com/2005/10/02/us/to-more-inmates-life-term-means-dying-behind-bars.html.

———. "Weighing Life in Prison for Youths Who Didn't Kill." *New York Times*, November 7, 2009. http://www.nytimes.com/2009/11/08/us/08juveniles.html.

Lopez, German. "America's Prisoners Are Going on Strike in at Least 17 States." *Vox*, August 22, 2018. https://www.vox.com/2018/8/17/17664048/national-prison-strike-2018.

———. "Congress's Prison Reform Bill, Explained." *Vox*, May 22, 2018. https://www.vox.com/policy-and-politics/2018/5/22/17377324/first-step-act-prison-reform-congress.

Lungren, Daniel E. "Victims and the Exclusionary Rule." *Harvard Journal of Law and Public Policy* (Spring 1996): 695–701.

Madrigal, Alexis C. "The Making of an Online Moral Crisis." *Atlantic*, June 19, 2018. https://www.theatlantic.com/technology/archive/2018/06/the-making-of-a-moral-problem/563114.

Mangan, Gregg. "Notorious New-Gate Prison." ConnecticutHistory.org. Accessed November 16, 2018. https://connecticuthistory.org/notorious-new-gate-prison.

Martin, Marlene. "What Happened to Prison Education Programs?" SocialistWorker.org, June 2, 2009. http://socialistworker.org/2009/06/02/what-happened-to-prison-education.

Martinez, Edecio. "Susan Atkins Death Peaceful Compared with Sharon Tate's." CBS News, September 25, 2009. http://www.cbsnews.com/8301-504083_162-5339017-504083.html.

Maynard, Gary. "Correctional Health Continues to Provide Quality Care." *Corrections Today* (October 2007).

McCarthy, Niall. "Report: The Number of People Serving Life Sentences in the U.S. Is Surging [Infographic]." Forbes, May 5, 2017. https://www.forbes.com/sites/niallmccarthy/2017/05/05/report-the-number-of-people-serving-life-sentences-in-the-u-s-is-surging-infographic/#3a486c69691d.

McGraw, Seamus. "Teen Boot Camp: A Deadly Decision?" *Reader's Digest*, June 2008.

McKillop, Matt. "Aging Prison Populations Drive Up Costs." Pew Charitable Trusts, February 20, 2018. https://www.pewtrusts.org/en/research-and-analysis/articles/2018/02/20/aging-prison-populations-drive-up-costs.

———. "Prison Health Care Spending Varies Dramatically by State." Pew Charitable Trusts, December 15, 2017. https://www.pewtrusts.org/en/research-and-analysis/articles/2017/12/15/prison-health-care-spending-varies-dramatically-by-state.

McNabb, Marianne. "Translating Research into Practice: Improving Safety in Women's Facilities." Department of Justice, December 2008.

Miroff, Nick, Josh Dawsey, and Maria Sacchetti. "Trump Administration Weighs New Family-Separation Effort at Border." *Washington Post*, October 12, 2018. https://www.washingtonpost.com/local/immigration/trump-administration-weighs-new-family-separation-effort-at-border/2018/10/12/45895cce-cd7b-11e8-920f-dd52e1ae4570_story.html?utm_term=.8ad2d8e4d6a0.

Moore, Solomon. "Mentally Ill Offenders Stretch the Limits of Juvenile Justice." *New York Times*, August 10, 2009. https://www.nytimes.com/2009/08/10/us/10juvenile.html.

Morgan, William J. "Correctional Officer Stress: A Review of the Literature, 1977–2007." *American Jails* (May/June 2009): 33–43.

———. "Study Finds Record Number of Inmates Serving Life." *New York Times*, July 23, 2009.

Morris, Roger. *The Devil's Butcher Shop: The New Mexico Prison Uprising*. Albuquerque, NM: University of New Mexico Press, 1983.

Muraskin, Roslyn, ed. *Key Correctional Issues*. Upper Saddle River, NJ: Pearson/Prentice Hall, 2005.

Myers, David. Boys *Among Men: Trying and Sentencing Juveniles as Adults*. New York: Praeger, 2005.

"National Prison Rape Elimination Commission Report." National Prison Rape Elimination Commission, 2009. https://www.ncjrs.gov/pdffiles1/226680.pdf.

Nebraska Juvenile Correctional Facilities Master Plan Update. June 2007. http://dhhs.ne.gov/documents/chinn.pdf.

Nellis, Ashley, and Ryan King. "No Exit." Sentencing Project, 2009.

"New Jersey Assembly Prison Gang Violence Task Force Final Report." New Jersey State Legislature, 2006.

Peterson, Iver. "Cutting Down on Amenities to Achieve No-Frills Jails." *New York Times*, July 10, 1995. https://www.nytimes.com/1995/07/10/nyregion/cutting-down-on-amenities-to-achieve-no-frills-jails.html.

Preston, Julia. "Lawyers Back Creating New Immigration Courts." *New York Times*, February 9, 2010. https://www.nytimes.com/2010/02/09/us/09immig.html.

"Prison Health Care Costs and Quality." Pew Charitable Trusts, October 18, 2017. https://www.pewtrusts.org/en/research-and-analysis/reports/2017/10/prison-health-care-costs-and-quality.

Public Opinion Strategies, Mellman Group. "Public Opinion on Sentencing and Corrections Policy in America." Pew Charitable Trusts, March 2012. https://www.pewtrusts.org/~/media/assets/2012/03/30/pew_nationalsurveyresearchpaper_final.pdf.

Rath, Arun. "Trump Inherits Guantanamo's Remaining Detainees." NPR, January 19, 2017. https://www.npr.org/2017/01/19/510448989/trump-inherits-guantanamos-remaining-detainees.

"Recidivism." National Institute of Justice, June 17, 2014. https://www.nij.gov/topics/corrections/recidivism/Pages/welcome.aspx.

"Reducing the Incarceration of Youth of Color in Berks County." Models for Change: Systems Reform in Juvenile Justice, May 13, 2009. http://modelsforchange.net/reform-progress/14.

Richards, Tori. "Upgrades to Illegal Immigrant Facilities Probed." AOL News, http://www.aolnews.com/article/proposed-ice-detention-center-upgrades-questioned/19534495.

Rivers, Eileen. "D.C. Youth Detention Emerges as Model of Improvement, but Struggles Persist." *USA TODAY*, December 30, 2017. https://www.usatoday.com/story/opinion/policing/reentry/column/2017/12/30/d-c-youth-detention-emerges-model-improvement-but-struggles-persist/978857001.

Roney, Marty. "36 States Release Ill or Dying Inmates." *USA TODAY*, August 14, 2008. http://www.usatoday.com/news/nation/2008-08-13-furloughs_N.htm.

Rothwell, Jonathan. "How the War on Drugs Damages Black Social Mobility." Brookings, September 30, 2014. https://www.brookings.edu/blog/social-mobility-memos/2014/09/30/how-the-war-on-drugs-damages-black-social-mobility.

Sawyer, Wendy. "Youth Confinement: The Whole Pie." Prison Policy Initiative, February 27, 2018. https://www.prisonpolicy.org/reports/youth2018.html.

Schemo, Diana Jean. "Report Recounts Horrors of Youth Boot Camps." *New York Times*, October 11, 2007. https://www.nytimes.com/2007/10/11/washington/11report.html.

Schnurer, Eric. "Shrinking Prisons: Good Crime-Fighting and Good Government." *Atlantic*, October 29, 2014. https://www.theatlantic.com/politics/archive/2014/10/shrinking-prisons-good-crime-fighting-and-good-government/381910.

Schoenherr, Steve. "Prison Reforms in American History." University of San Diego, November 30, 2009. http://history.sandiego.edu/gen/soc/prison.html.

Schuppe, Jon. "Criminal Justice Reform Finally Has a Chance in Congress. Here's What the First Step Act Would Do." NBC News, November 15, 2018 https://www.nbcnews.com/news/us-news/criminal-justice-reform-finally-has-chance-congress-here-s-what-n936866.

Schwartz, Sunny, and David Boodell. *Dreams from the Monster Factory: A Tale of Prison, Redemption and One Woman's Fight to Restore Justice to All.* New York: Scribner, 2009.

"Second Chance Act Grant Program." National Reentry Resource Center. Accessed November 17, 2018. https://csgjusticecenter.org/nrrc/projects/second-chance-act.

Senate Judiciary Committee. "Reducing Recidivism at the Local Level." Congressional testimony of Amy Solomon, November 5, 2009.

Soering, Jens. "Life Without Parole." *Christian Century*, August 12, 2008. https://www.christiancentury.org/article/2008-08/life-without-parole.

"Still Life: America's Increasing Use of Life and Long-Term Sentences." Sentencing Project, 2017. https://www.sentencingproject.org/wp-content/uploads/2017/05/Still-Life.pdf.

Talbot, Margaret. "The Lost Children." *New Yorker*, March 3, 2008. https://www.newyorker.com/magazine/2008/03/03/the-lost-children.

Tartaro, Christine. "Are They Really Direct Supervision Jails?" *American Jails* (November/December 2006): 9–16.

Tartaro, Christine, and Marissa Levy. "Crowding, Violence and Direct Supervision Jails." *American Jails* (September/October 2008): 12–22.

"Thirteen States Have No Minimum Age for Adult Prosecution of Children." Equal Justice Initiative, September 19, 2016. https://eji.org/news/13-states-lack-minimum-age-for-trying-kids-as-adults.

Travis, Jeremy, Bruce Western, and Steve Redburn, Eds. *The Growth of Incarceration in the United States: Exploring Causes and Consequences.* Washington, DC: National Academies Press, 2014. https://www.nap.edu/catalog/18613/the-growth-of-incarceration-in-the-united-states-exploring-causes.

"United States." Global Detention Project. Accessed November 18, 2018. https://www.globaldetentionproject.org/countries/americas/united-states.

"US: Immigration Detention Neglects Health." Human Rights Watch, March 17, 2009. https://www.hrw.org/news/2009/03/17/us-immigration-detention-neglects-health.

"US: Poor Medical Care, Deaths, in Immigrant Detention." Human Rights Watch, June 20, 2018. https://www.hrw.org/news/2018/06/20/us-poor-medical-care-deaths-immigrant-detention.

Wagner, Peter, and Wendy Sawyer. "Mass Incarceration: The Whole Pie 2018." Prison Policy Initiative, March 14, 2018. https://www.prisonpolicy.org/reports/pie2018.html.

Williams, Timothy. "Inside a Private Prison: Blood, Suicide and Poorly Paid Guards." *New York Times*, April 3, 2018. https://www.nytimes.com/2018/04/03/us/mississippi-private-prison-abuse.html.

Winton, Richard, and Hector Becerra. "Manson Follower Susan Atkins Is Denied Parole." *Los Angeles Times*, September 3, 2009. http://articles.latimes.com/2009/sep/03/local/me-susan-atkins3.

Woo, Elaine. "Susan Atkins Dies at 61; Imprisoned Charles Manson Follower." *Los Angeles Times*, September 26, 2009. http://www.latimes.com/news/obituaries/la-me-susan-atkins26-2009sep26,0,4180642.story?page=1.

Yurcaba, Josephine. "For Survivors of Prison Rape, Saying 'Me Too' Isn't an Option." *Rewire.News*, January 8, 2018. https://rewire.news/article/2018/01/08/survivors-prison-rape-saying-isnt-option.

——— "Rape Behind Bars: Stopping the Cycle of Violence." Nation Swell, September 28, 2018. http://nationswell.com/rape-in-prison.

Zweig, Janine M., and John Blackmore. "Strategies to Prevent Prison Rape." *NIJ Journal* (October 2008): 1–10.

Index

About the Authors

Erin L. McCoy is a literature, language, and cultural studies educator and an award-winning photojournalist and poet. She holds a master of arts degree in Hispanic studies and a master of fine arts degree in creative writing from the University of Washington. She has edited more than two dozen nonfiction books for young adults, including *The Mexican-American War*, *The Israel-Palestine Border Conflict*, and *Poverty: Public Crisis or Private Struggle?* from Cavendish Square Publishing. She is from Louisville, Kentucky.

Jeff Burlingame is the award-winning author of roughly twenty books, including *The Lost Boys of Sudan* in the Great Escapes series. In 2011, his book on Malcolm X was nominated for an NAACP Image Award for Outstanding Literary Work—Youth and Teens. Before becoming a full-time author, Burlingame was a writer and an editor for various newspapers and magazines. Among the books he's written are *The Titanic Tragedy* in the Perspectives On series and *Government Entitlements*. He resides with his family in Washington State.